Assembly Line Balance

Practical Industrial Engineering
in the Documentation,
Measurement, and Balance
of the Assembly Line

by

Tom Shropshire

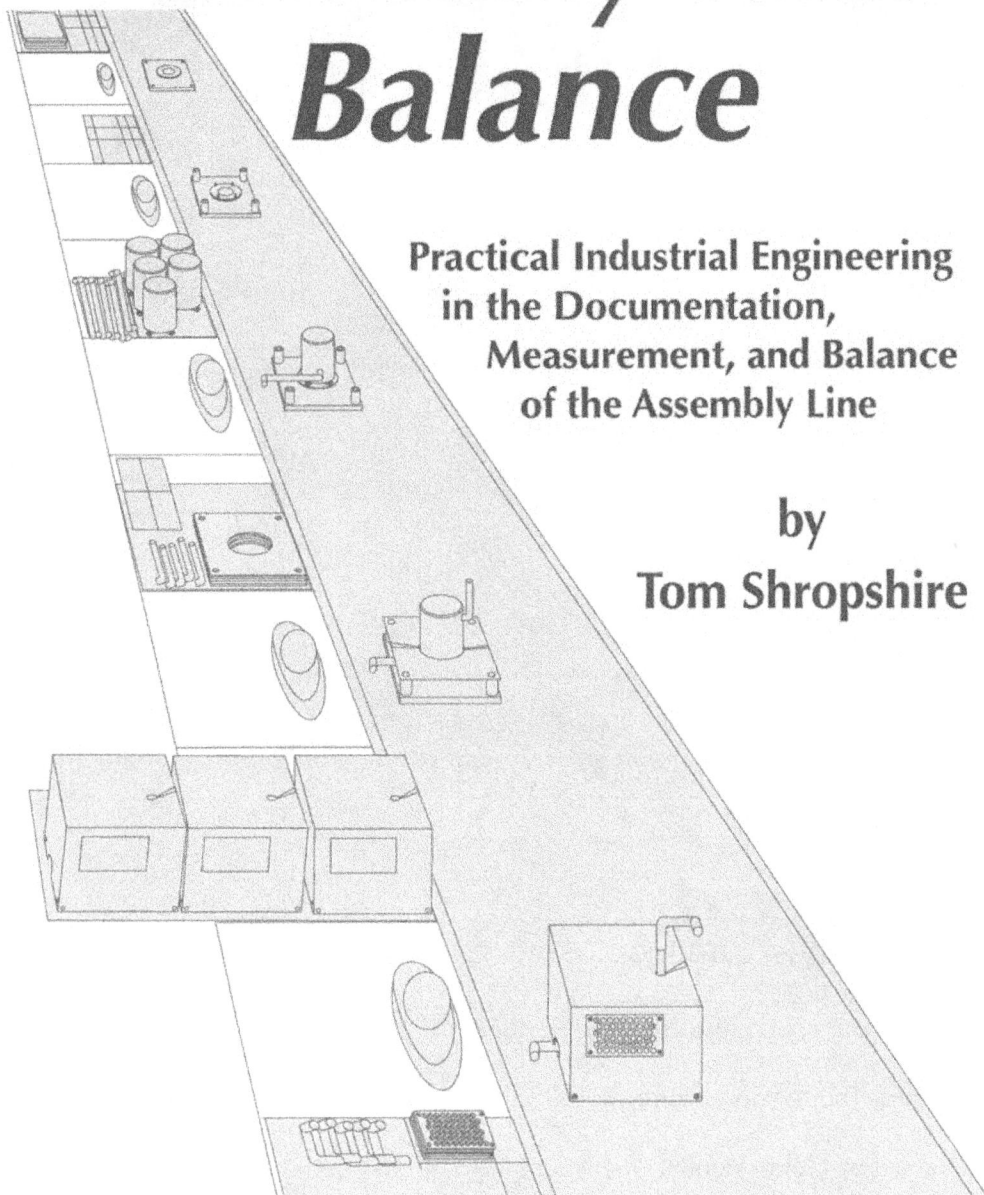

Published by Thomas Shropshire
ISBN: 978-0-9968721-2-6
Library of Congress Control No: 2018908686

Copyright © Thomas Shropshire, 2018

Book layout by Guido Henkel

Table of Contents

Foreword—Solving the Puzzle

For many years I've commented on the fact that people like to solve puzzles. They visit drugstores, and supermarket checkout lines, and other venues to buy magazines and books devoted exclusively to puzzles. From word search to Sudoku to the venerable crossword, people are willing to spend their money, and their time, working out solutions for which there is no reward, other than the satisfaction of doing so.

They will buy newspapers, sometimes with no interest in the content other than the amusements page. Likewise, patrons at morning coffee shops will look for the "house" paper, to see if anyone has yet gotten to the puzzles. But I belabor this obvious truth.

I do so because I gloat over the fact that while others go to sometimes great lengths to solve puzzles, merely for their own satisfaction and amusement, I on the other hand have for many years been *paid* to solve puzzles. It is the nature of the Industrial Engineering profession to find solutions to those puzzlers which are presented daily in any manufacturing environment.

One of my favorite jokes, which I heard many years ago, tells a tale of the French Revolution, and of three men riding the cart to the guillotine.

A priest, a philosopher, and an Industrial Engineer arrived at the scaffold to meet their fate. Each, in turn, was asked one question. "Do you choose to be positioned in the stocks facing up, or facing down?"

First, the priest. When asked this question, he went on for some time explaining why it was better to face heaven, rather than to be placed in the opposite position. When at last he was secured, face up, and the lanyard was pulled, the blade descended about half way, and stopped! Amazement swept through the crowd, and the consensus was that he was indeed a holy man, and that God had spared him, and that he should be released.

Next, the philosopher, who had been paying close attention. He explained, at great length the philosophical reasoning for choosing to be placed face up. When, finally, the philosopher was positioned and the lanyard pulled, the blade once again descended halfway, and stopped. Once again, the crowd was amazed, and felt that his reasoning was so pure that he too should be spared.

Next, the third member of our trio. It is widely accepted that Industrial Engineers are quick studies, and this one was no exception. Without ado he chose to be placed face up, and was positioned so in the stocks. In his final moments took the opportunity to examine the mechanism. To the amazement of the crowd, before the lanyard could be pulled, he cried out "Hey, there's the problem!"

And so it is, we Industrial Engineers are by profession, and by nature, solvers of puzzles. And as for me, I feel there can be no more satisfying puzzle to solve than the successful balance of a manufacturing process, in the form of a production assembly line.

Whether a simple, two person synchronous assembly process, or a long, incredibly complex, mixed model line which can expel a series of complete automobiles—each in less than a minute—assembly lines are puzzles. And we get to solve them.

We've taken a brief look at who we are. The remainder of this book will focus on what we do, and how we do it. Not from an academic perspective, or a theoretical perspective; but instead we will spend our time with those things which we need to know, the skills we must have, and the techniques we apply in the actual practice of Industrial Engineering on the shop floor.

Part One

The Necessity of Documentation

1. Building Blocks

Introduction

This book assumes, for the most part, that you are encountering an established assembly process, running on an existing assembly-line. However, the possible circumstances of your project are many and varied—from a mature process needing only a rebalance due to change in demand, to a newly constituted line, and a beta process needing organization and refinement in all aspects.

Many years ago, when I was an industrial engineer at Harley Davidson in Milwaukee, the daily demand for engine/transmission units—determined by marketing—was revised several times each week. Each new number of required engine units per day necessitated a change in the number of workstations on which they were assembled. More for higher volumes, less for decreased demand.

Most of what was needed of course already existed. Elements of work and their time values had long since been determined. Tooling and equipment already existed and needed only to be re-located as required. What did not exist was the true heart of the exercise. Elements of work needed to be reassigned, and time leveled, over a different number of workstations—In other words, a line balance.

At the extreme other end of the scale is a new assembly line—often developed by a Manufacturing Engineer (either highly skilled, or not so much), a build sequence almost certainly not optimized, and assembly practices which fall well short of the notion of "best methods".

Any given assignment you are likely to receive to "rebalance that line" will fall somewhere between these two extremes. Therefore for the purposes of this book we will focus on a circumstance somewhere in the middle.

In any case, the ultimate goal is a well-balanced assembly process. The methodologies by which we accomplish that balance are offered here. And it all starts with something called the Sequence of Events.

The Sequence of Events

I want to begin with a jab at the attitude of many "non-Industrial Engineer" lean practitioners and the current passion for LEAN in American business and manufacturing. A few years ago, in one of the many LinkedIN group discussions on Industrial Engineering topics, participants were asked to comment on "How labor standards, and the determination of the elements of each operation is the root development of lean practices …"

My response was; "The fundamental, then detailed understanding of a manufacturing process, as defined by its sequence of work elements is a core principle in Industrial Engineering, and yes, absolutely essential in the practice of LEAN".

But the determination of elemental sequence is *not* a new age development, or a derivative of LEAN. In the Industrial Engineering world, we have known—long before there was LEAN—that defining the basic sequence of work elements is *the* fundamental step in the analytical process used to do the things we will discuss in this book, and in fact, virtually all Industrial Engineering practices.

IEs have known for a very long time that this "Sequence of Events"—what in the world of LEAN is these days often referred to as "Standard Work", is the base from which *everything* flows. The Sequence of Events (or Work Elements) is not merely a sequential, description of work content. Derived, or sometimes inferred, from the Sequence of Events comes work station, cell, or line layout, as well as required tooling and equipment. Material presentation, in fact the entire Supply Chain is, in many ways determined by the "Pull" of the elemental assembly steps which consume that material.

And of course, principle among these derivatives is *time*. Process time; from which flows balance of process, staffing and labor cost, scheduling and on-time delivery, and so on.

The Sequence of Events: A Macro View

In this section we will be discussing the basic documentation of an assembly process. The sequence of events *concept*, however applies at all levels of analysis. At the Macro level for example, the popular term "supply chain", represented by the simplified and hypothetical flow diagram below, can be documented as a Sequence of Events:

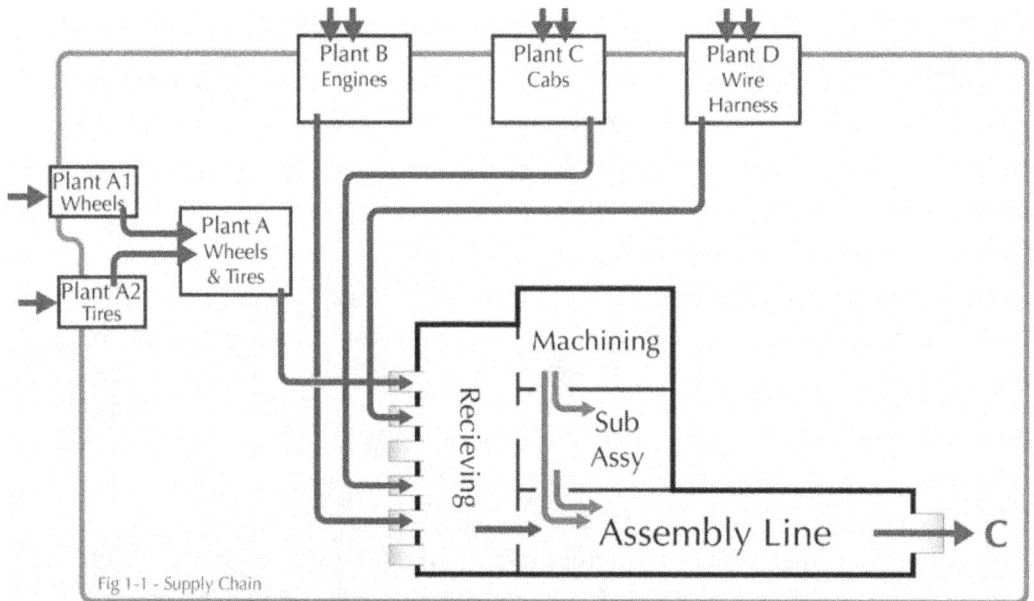

Fig 1-1 - Supply Chain

The movement, consumption, and transformation of component materials into sub-assemblies or completed products represented here would be documented as a series of discrete events:

1. Delivery of Wheels from Plant A1 to Plant A
2. Delivery of Tires from Plant A2 to Plant A
3. Mounting of Tires to Wheels (Plant A)
4. Delivery of Mounted Tires from Plant A to Receiving Dock (Final Assembly Plant)
5. Delivery of Engines from Plant B to Receiving Dock
6. Delivery of Cabs from Plant C to Receiving Dock
7. Delivery of Wire Harnesses from Plant D to Receiving Dock
8. Production of Fabricated Components
9. Delivery of Fabricated Components to Sub-Assembly
10. Delivery of Fabricated Components to Assembly Line Stations
11. Conversion of (some) Fabricated Components into Sub-Assemblies
12. Delivery of Sub-Assemblies to Assembly Line Stations
13. Delivery of Supplies, and Components (Engines, Cabs, etc.) to Assembly Line Stations
14. Assembly of Product at Assembly Line Stations
15. Delivery of Product to Customer(s) (C)

An important thing to note in this example is that not only does this view clarify an otherwise complex process, but allows for the recognition and timing of each discreet event. Further, if we were to introduce a timeline, we would notice that some events may happen simultaneously, while others are dependent on the completion of some other activity before they themselves can occur. A very great deal of organizational and management information may be inferred from a simple in-sequence listing of activities.

Authors Note: Sequence of Events is the most common term used to describe a listing of process activities. As we go forward I will continue to use the term Sequence of Events when referencing the overall list, but will use the word "Elements' when speaking of specific items which make up the list. Simply said, in this case the terms "Events" and Elements" are synonymous.

The Sequence of Events: A Micro View

At the extreme other end of the scale is the Sequence of Events at the "Micro" level. The following is an MTM (Methods-Time-Measurement) analysis of a simple sequence of work elements. MTM is still used today to document and precisely measure sometimes complex, short cycle work. An example of a micro level documentation (and in this case measurement) of this task might look like this:

Place Pencil to Tray & Move Tray to Rear of Desktop

1	Obtain Pencil from Desktop and Place to Tray			28.2
a.	Reach 13" to Pencil	R-HA-13"	8.9	
b.	Grasp Pencil w/Thumb and (2) Fingers	G-1A	2.0	
c.	Move Pencil 8" to Tray	M-A-8"	9.7	
d.	Position Pencil to center section of Tray	P-1S	5.6	
e.	Release Pencil	V1-1	2.0	
2	Slide Tray to Rear of Desktop			34.9
a.	Reach 4" to edge of Tray	R-HA-4"	4.9	
b.	Contact Tray w/Hand	G-5	0.0	
c.	Slide Tray w/Hand 16" to rear of Desktop	M-B-16"	15.8	
d.	Release Tray	V1-2	0.0	
e.	Return Hand to starting position - 18"	R-HA-18"	14.2	
	Total TMU:			**63.1**

Fig 1-2 - MTM

For the moment, we are still discussing the overall *concept* of the SOE. So, if we break down the analysis above, we will find not one, but three sequences.

The overall task is defined by the Element title "Place Pencil in Tray and Relocate Tray to Rear of Desktop". The two components of this element "Move Pencil to Tray" and "Aside Tray" list and define the steps required to accomplish the task. This is an, albeit very simple, two step Sequence of Events.

Place Pencil in Tray and Relocate Tray to Rear of Desktop

1. Obtain Pencil from Desktop and Place to Tray
2. Slide Tray to Rear of Desktop

A further breakdown of motions in the MTM "method and time analysis" reveals that each component element has its own sequence of components—these at perhaps the lowest possible level. Using this example, we can see that each of the two component elements of the overall Sequence of Events are in fact, descriptive titles of work detailed in the method and time analysis.

So the concept of the Sequence of Events is shown at its lowest level where, in this case, not only is the work detailed, but timed as well. As you can see, the *concept,* and the technique of sequence of events documentation is applicable to virtually any work flow analysis, at any level.

Using the Sequence of Events

I have stated that the sequence of events is the basis for all things, or at least all things Industrial Engineering. And we have now spent some time discussing the concept of the sequence of events and how it is structured. We will discuss, a bit later, how to actually create a sequence of events for a real process. Before we do, let's spend a bit of time talking about what we do with—and how we actually use —the sequence of events. And why I think it's so important.

The sequence of events which you generate for your assembly process can be, or can become, many things. First, foremost—and I would think most obviously—it is a simple, start to finish, listing of all of the work elements required to assemble a product. Including how much time each step in that process is expected to take; the sum of which, "Total Work Content", is the amount of time required to build the complete assembly. As we will see later, this bit of information is critical to the organization of the line on which the product will run.

To organize, and especially to balance, the process elements, it is absolutely vital to know and to understand the actual work represented by each element. The sequence of events is, or should be, written in the order of assembly, as observed. To further divide the completed list into individual workstations is simple. But to "Balance" the process, one or more individual work elements (represented as blocks of *time*) must be moved (re-assigned) between work stations, while still maintaining the *linear integrity* of the process. *(In other words, you cannot assign the Engine Cover to anywhere in the process prior to installing the Engine).*

Achieving this may prove difficult if the person balancing has a poor, or incomplete understanding of the relationships between elements, as well as their limitations and/or dependencies. Fortunately, I have found that the process of generating and documenting the sequence of events, helps very much to fix this information in my mind. And we will discuss this process at some length in the following pages.

The elemental steps of the sequence will, in all likelihood, be elaborated upon—to whatever level of detail is desired—at a later time by adding required tools, parts, instructional notes, etc. The sequence of events may be revised into Standard Work (used in the management of the line), or as Work Instructions (for the line associates). Or very often both. The completed sequence of events often becomes the complete repository for *all* manufacturing information related to that product, on that line.

Once the basic listing of assembly steps (elements) is complete, all additional information is added at the elemental level. This provides for discrete lists showing where and when specific items and information are needed. For example: A Bill of Material organized by "Where Used", showing not only Work Station but perhaps even specific Bin locations and Kanban Quantities.

An additional benefit to this is, if and when the line is rebalanced yet again, and elements are re-assigned to different work stations, all of that discrete manufacturing information is automatically moved with them.

Work Element Structure—Scope and Content

As we have seen, elements may represent any type of work or activity, and may be seen and documented at any level, as a single analysis, or any combination of smaller more detailed studies. From this point forward we will consider the Sequence of Events only as it applies to the series of discreet events which comprise the assembly line process.

From the first to the last, the assembly-line sequence of events is a listing of all assembly steps (Elements) which, in total, comprise the complete process. These elements not only describe each assembly step in sequence, but also define their **Scope**.

The scope of each element, in simple terms, is the size of the element, as measured by the amount of work performed, (the **Content**) and is defined by its first action to its last action, and of course what lies between. Where each element begins and ends, in documentation, is determined by the analyst. Elemental scope (or size) depends on two things. The nature of the product, and the desired accuracy required when the work is measured.

In documenting the assembly of electronic circuit board, for example, each whole element of work may be comparable to our previous example, and the entire process (with individual work stations being just seconds in duration) perhaps analyzed and measured with a tool such as MTM .

An assembly line producing farm tractors, on the other hand operates on a different scale. A single work element may be as large as "Mount Left Side Rear Wheel", which would consist of hundreds of tiny, but measurable motions, but which may be documented, analyzed and measured with a somewhat broader tool—such as Time Study, or a Predetermined Time System (such as M.O.S.T), or Standard Data, while maintaining acceptable accuracy

Break Points

The key to establishing the scope of each element lies in determining where one ends, and the next begins. This moment in the flow of work is known as a **Break Point**.

Break Points can occasionally be a bit obscure, but for the most part are rather easy to recognize. In the simplest terms the break point is that instant when the last action of an element is completed, and the first action of the next element begins.

Pauses, unnecessary actions, or delays of one kind or another may sometimes attempt to blur the line, but the precise moment a Break Point occurs can be easily recognized with further, careful observations. Additional, unnecessary motions are dismissed and thereafter ignored.

Correctly established, break points are essential in the establishment of the sequence of events, and later, in elemental time measurement. Break points – *those moments the watch is "clicked", either metaphorically, or in reality*—are vitally important in generating accurate times.

The Smallest Transferable Element

Based upon circumstances, and the desired outcome, the scope of each element should follow the basic, and rather simplistic, principle of being neither too small, nor too large. Generally, elemental scope should adhere to a basic rule. That each element represents the *"Smallest Transferable Whole Task"*. In other words, the smallest complete element of work which may be (in balancing) reassigned to another workstation.

Consider, as an example, the following task, observed as a single series of actions:

Obtain (2) Hydraulic Tubes. Position Tubes to Inside/Left wall of Frame and attach w/(3) Dual P-Clamps. Tighten P-Clamps w/Power Tool.

Even though this work is performed, in sequence, by one person, it must be documented, in the sequence of events, as two discreet elements.

Element 1—Loose assemble (2) Hydraulic Tubes to Frame w/(3) P-Clamps

Element 2—Tighten (3) L/S Hydr Tube P-Clamp Screws w/Power Tool

After the Tubes are clamped to the Frame Wall, the three Screws *may* be immediately tightened. However, it may be necessary to reorganize the sequence (re-balance) and assign a portion of that task to another station. It is not *necessary* to tighten the Clamp hardware at that time. Final tightening of the Screws is, therefore, is itself a whole, complete—and importantly—transferable element of work.

I belabor the obvious, but simply positioning the Tubes to the side wall, without at least *loose* assembling the Clamps and Screws is NOT a whole, complete task.

Also note that it is important to that each element title adequately describe the scope of its work content. Read as successive items on a list, it would be easy to infer that Element 2 is the tightening the three Clamps just installed. However, if that element is later moved to a different work station, this action would now take place within a series of untreated events, and the element description must be full and complete.

To carry this example just a bit further, if the fasteners needed to be torqued, this also would be a complete transferable event. The entire activity, assembly and hardware, tightening, and torqueing, may well occur in sequence at a single workstation, or may occur in one or more stations further down the line.

2. Knowing the Product

"If you don't have a good understanding of how the finished process should look, it is much more difficult to make good decisions about the individual methods. Get a big picture view with some upfront analysis and planning"

Lean Workplace Series "Best Methods"
© 2000 HB Maynard & Co

Learning the Product Mix

I suppose I have talked enough about the concept and the nature of the generic sequence of events, and the elements which comprise the list. Now it is time to talk about how to actually gather information and generate Process Documentation. Surprisingly perhaps, other than the initial, basic familiarization of the line—the physical environment in which the work is occurring—the documentation process does *not* begin on the shop floor. Prior to documenting the elements of an assembly sequence, and the specifics of those process steps, it is necessary to gain an understanding of the entire product, with all its variations and complexities.

Seldom does just *one thing* go down an assembly line. The very common term "Mixed Model Assembly Line" may very probably describe the situation with which you are confronted. A line may produce a single product configuration, but more likely a product with variations (Customer or Model Options), or a line may produce multiple products—each, perhaps, with *their own* model options.

A line assembling Lawn Mowers, for example will be likely to include mowers of several sizes—i.e. Small, Medium, Large. Each of these sizes may have variations, such as different engine sizes, different blade lengths, or a hand-propelled mower vs. powered drive. Options may be mechanically complex, or as simple as a different color.

Available Resources

A necessary part of your preparation for learning, documenting, and ultimately balancing, an assembly process is to understand the universe of possibilities which you may encounter when you do so.

Beyond initially going to the line and watching a few cycles at each work station (an activity which I strongly encourage you to do), there are additional resources available to help you learn the product "mix", and also to help shed light on some of the more confusing, or possibly incomprehensible things that you may have seen in your initial observations. Among the product information to which you should automatically have access, of course, are assembly drawings and bills of material (parts lists). Additional helpful resources, which are sometimes overlooked, are Service Parts Books, and often most valuable of all, Product Brochures, Specification and Data Sheets.

I have a belief that product engineers (the designers) speak their own language—Engineeringese, perhaps—and tend to generate information which is rendered, and formatted for their own purposes. It is all perfectly clear to the authors of this information, so it must therefore be perfectly clear to everyone else. I have often said that a necessary function of the Industrial Engineer is to act as interpreter, taking the time to decipher engineering information, and to present it in a way—usually as a work instruction—that is easily and, most importantly, quickly understandable to those who actually build the product, and whose time is valuable.

Product brochures, on the other hand, are developed by marketing—specifically for customers. This literature can also be of great value to the Industrial Engineer in gaining the required product knowledge. While this material contains a lot of technical information, product brochures are generally written to explain the product—and all its variations and options—in a comparatively simple fashion, allowing potential customers to select and order the specific model and configuration suitable to their needs.

This material will also certainly show *you* all of the product mix possibilities, and help you to understand them. These items often make information, which is often buried deep in assembly drawings and BOMs, readily available. Information which is invaluable in acquiring product knowledge, understanding product variations, and organizing and structuring process documentation.

For example: For a line producing Lawn Mowers, you may find that a Mechanical Drive option is only available with the largest Engine choice, and which Blades are available with which Engines, and so on.

Additionally, Service Parts Manuals contain parts lists organized by base components and model options, and contain exploded view drawings which will be very helpful to your understanding of just how the product is built, and by extension, the methods and the tools required to do so.

The Product Matrix

Digging into this information will provide you with a wealth of information. From this data, I turn to MS Excel to create an organizational tool which I call the "Product Matrix". For the above mentioned (hypothetical) Lawn Mower assembly line, the resulting Product Matrix might look something like this:

			Residential Lawn Mower Line									
	Series:		Small	Medium								Large
	Model:		125	225	275	325		375		425		525
			2.5 HP	4 HP	5.5 HP	6 HP	6 HP	7 HP		8 HP		10 HP
			Hand	Hand	Hand	Power	Hand	Hand	Power	Hand	Power	Power
1 Blade		No Mulch										
		w/Mulch										
2 Blade	Reg Wheels	No Mulch										
		w/Mulch										
	Large Wheels	No Mulch										
		w/Mulch										
3 Blade	Reg Wheels	No Mulch										
		w/Mulch										
	Large Wheels	No Mulch										
		w/Mulch										

Fig 1-3 Product Matrix

Authors Note: Before the days of the PC, I used to do this with graph paper and a pencil. It was always quite exasperating to discover, the need for an additional line or column after I thought I had it all. Believe me, Excel is better.

Starting with the basic configurations, product attributes are organized on the top and side axis. As details of the product variations are identified new columns and/ or rows are added. The Matrix, when complete will encompass the entire universe of product option *possibilities*. Each box of the matrix represents a unique model configuration.

A review of the product literature will quickly show boxes representing impossible combinations. These boxes are shaded, and thereafter ignored. A close reading of product data sheets will likewise reveal options which, while possible, are just not offered. These boxes are also grayed out. The remaining boxes of the matrix display all of the possible model configurations which will, or may, actually run on the assembly-line.

The boxes of the product matrix do not represent process information, but rather identify where process information is required, and for what. I whimsically refer to this as first identifying and creating all of the required "holes", and then systematically filling them with data. Some of these holes will represent significant variations, while some may represent a process virtually identical to its neighbors, with but one or two differences. Regardless of product option complexity, a properly constructed and complete matrix is extremely helpful in seeing, and understanding, the "mix".

When beginning data collection, armed with this fore-knowledge, and you observe elements of the process which you know to be an option, you will know that on some models, that work will not be performed, or perhaps different work will be required. Conversely, if the model you are observing does not include a known option, you know what questions to ask. As we will discuss a bit later, asking the right questions can be a key factor to success. "Knowledge is power".

I find the product matrix to be an invaluable starting point. But for me, an additional benefit is that I find the exercise of researching the options and creating a complete matrix helps fix the information in my mind. Occasionally, while creating the matrix, if something in the literature seems confusing, a review of the Service Parts Manual, or a trip to the line with a question or two usually provides an "Aha, so that's how it works" answer.

Paralysis by Analysis

Initial observations on the line notwithstanding, I've been continually surprised over the years at how many people want to just march out to the floor and start "writing things down" with no real grasp of what they're dealing with. My advice is to take a bit of time up front and learn as much as you can about the product. Then on your trips to the floor you can test what you think you know against the reality of what you find. Usually these are very nearly the same thing, but the trip is worth it.

Researching and creating the matrix allows you to consider and map every possibility and later discard combinations which doesn't exist; a process which I find in the long run to be more productive than formalizing your data only to discover holes, or extra "stuff" for which you have not planned.

Over the years I've occasionally been questioned for not immediately "getting out there, and getting to it". But I've always been vindicated in the end, when thorough preparation led to fast, generally correction-free completions.

There is a limit however. It is possible to endlessly gather information, without ever actually doing anything. There's a term for this: Paralysis by Analysis.

3. Learning the Process

Get Out There and Get To It

Once you have a good grasp of the product, the time has come to "*Get Out There, and Get To It*".

In other words, go to the line and poke around, (without getting in the way). Follow the unit(s)—which you are now familiar with—from the obtain of the first part, to the end of the line, and just absorb the activity—and especially the environment. As I suggested earlier, it is important to have already been there a time or two. Often the experience of being in a new environment; noisy, fast-paced, initially hectic and confusing, and perhaps even uncomfortably hot, can, until you become acclimated, severely diminish your ability to see the things that are going on. So by the time you show up to start documenting what you see, you should be somewhat comfortable in the place in which you do so.

And remember, seeing, learning, and documenting is your *primary purpose* for being there. So, once again, take the time to watch, listen, and learn as you get comfortable being where you are. Knowing both the environment, and the people you will be interacting with, will be a big help in learning the process.

Also, I find it very valuable to walk the line, "After Hours". With the line idle, you can really get in and poke around. You can take your time; stick your hands, or perhaps your head, inside a partially assembled unit—without getting in anyone's way. As you walk the line, station- by-station, you will see, at your own pace, what parts have been added, and where. You can also, as I like to do, dig into the material bins, fondle the parts, and play around a bit. Discover on your own how some of the sub-assemblies go together. This is another great opportunity to match reality against what the product literature has shown you.

Just a bit later, when you are both observing, *and at the same time* writing down what you see, every bit of fore-knowledge will prove quite valuable.

Seeing the Mountain

A sailing student once said something to me which I thought was quite profound. "Learning to sail", she said, "was like learning to climb a mountain".

At first, you see just the mountain, and then, as you learn not to be intimidated by the magnitude of it, you begin to gain an understanding of, and an appreciation for, the task at hand. Then, armed with that knowledge, you start to think about what equipment might be necessary to get you to the top. *Then*, properly prepared and equipped, you begin to see the routes which may take you there. In time, focus narrows to the texture of the rock, the cracks, crevices, and outcroppings that you will exploit. She said that sailing was a bit like that. The first thing she saw was great big scary Lake Michigan, then the boat, then... Her first lesson, she later confided, had been mostly about just being there, and learning not to be nervous as the boat moved around in strange and unexpected ways. Achieving that, she quickly began to learn.

And that's the sequence I encourage you to follow as well. In the beginning, focus will be the line, and the assembly process—in its entirety. Once the actual documentation process begins, focus will be on one workstation at a time, and perspective is necessarily limited.

So before that happens, take a notepad and pen and walk the line, from Station One to the end. You may also—as I usually do—sketch a map of the line, identifying station locations, and introducing yourself to the assemblers within. And as you recognize discrete workstations, take a moment to name them. Assign to each station a simple description of what seems to be the principal activity.

Each work station will have something by which it can be identified. Some examples:

> Station 1—Load Frame to Line
>
> Station 5—Primary Wiring Station
>
> Station 12—Functional Test
>
> Station 14—Packing

The purpose of this exercise is to allow you to see the "mountain". The overall multi-station entity through which the assembly process—element by element, station by station—flows. There is much to learn from this macro view that will be useful to you as you go forward. Such things as where materials are positioned at the various workstations. Questions like, are there "feeder" operations, supplying subassemblies to the line, which may—or may not—fall within the parameters of your ultimate balance. And importantly when you're ready to begin documenting the work content of each of the work stations, you will know where they are.

Multi-Person Work Stations

It is unfortunate, but the term "Work Station" is almost universally applied to two different things—often within the same context. Work station can mean a physical location where work is performed (such as Station #3 of an assembly line—where tools, equipment, and component parts are located, and through which the units pass on their way down the line). Or it can be used, in the sense of line organization and balance to mean the place where work elements (and their time values, are assigned. This later refers to the person at a location doing the actual work.

When you encounter a single work station (location) to which multiple persons have been assigned, it is important to remember that no matter how work areas are officially designated, for the purpose of your analysis, and for the ultimate balance, *each person represents one work station*. For example, you may come to a place, or area on the line officially known as Station 3. Working within Station 3 are four assemblers—two on the right side of the line and two on the left.

Again what you are seeing and documenting are four individual entities to which work is assigned. In other words – *four Work Stations*. For purposes of identification

I would designate these individuals as Stations 3-1, 3-2, etc. Or perhaps—for more clarity—as 3-1R, 3-2R, 3-3L, and 3-4L, as shown below.

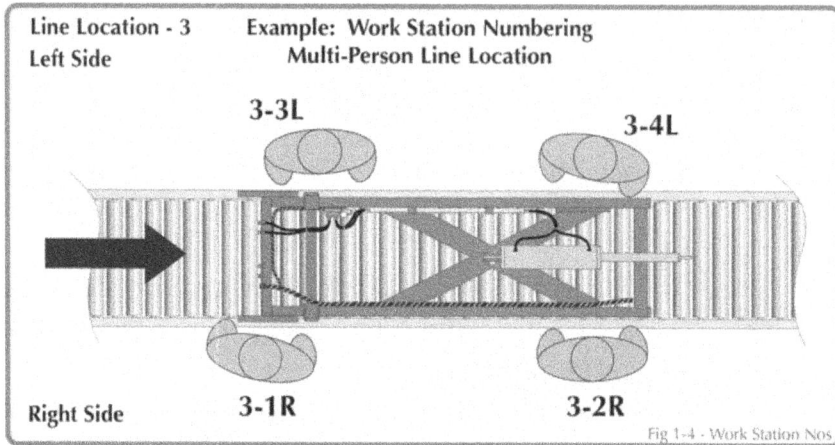

Fig 1-4 · Work Station Nos

It really doesn't matter what numbering system is used. What is important is to recognize and identify each individual as an entity to which work is, or may be assigned. Observe, and document, each person one at a time. With apologies for the gender bias in the language, I will borrow a football or basketball term; "Play the Man, Not the Zone".

In an effort to save engineering time, attempts are occasionally made to record the work activities of all persons within a Work Station (location) simultaneously, regardless of who is doing what. Referring to an old-time English expression, this effort virtually always "ends in tears".

Work Flow Patterns

I've often said that Industrial Engineers need to be quick studies and to have, or develop, the ability to enter a new situation, or environment, to recognize activities and patterns within what seems to be chaos. And to do so in a reasonable amount of time. Remember, each person is, with each new unit, doing—subject to variations within fairly close boundaries—exactly the same thing, so patterns will quickly appear.

Upon initial viewing an assembly work station can appear to be a confusing jumble of seemingly random activities. In particular, a multi-station, multi-person per station assembly line may well take that confusion to another level—total chaos. Multiple individuals are scurrying about in more or less the same space, sometimes interacting with each other, doing things which, seen in isolation, often make no sense. As we have discussed, it is almost *always* necessary to watch more than one cycle before patterns begin to emerge.

But emerge they will. Additional observations will reveal the same people, doing the same things, time after time. Some of those things may still not make sense, but a few more observation cycles, and perhaps a question or two, will soon make these activities identifiable, in context, as parts of a stable process.

Well-functioning work stations, even multi-person work stations, turn out, after all, to be not just a bunch of individuals scurrying about doing their own thing. You will quickly see that whether joining forces to accomplish a single task, or working solo, the overall activity of each individual is carefully choreographed. Rarely does one assembler bump into, or get in the way of another, or fail to be in the right place at the right time to "assist" in some shared task.

This work method you see *may* have been established by some talented Industrial Engineer, but it is also quite likely to have been organized by the team members themselves. In any case there are clear, repetitive patterns. To see and appreciate these patterns, it is necessary to see each person as an individual, and *then* as a member of the overall team.

Required Tools

So what tools do you need to create a Sequence of Events? Obviously if you're going out to just look, as part of your preparation, and to get a sense of what's going on, a notepad and pen are really all you need. Being old, and coming from a different era, I tend to believe that pen and paper are all you ever *really* need; something we will discuss in a moment.

Author's Note: Unless you're actually planning to capture the time of a specific activity, having a stopwatch with you is not only unnecessary, but if is visible may very well be counterproductive. We will talk in Part Two about the etiquettes, and protocols of actually timing people at their work.

— Pen and Paper (the Old-Fashioned Way)

For actual documentation, the technique of first videotaping a process, returning to the office, then viewing the tape and recording what you see is by far the most popular method these days. It is certainly the most comfortable of methodologies—especially if someone else does the actual taping. And taping is also considered by many to be the most efficient.

I tend to disagree. From this, you will probably conclude that I'm very old and have barely made it into the 21st century. There is probably a nugget of truth in this. But while I might not have thought so at the time, I feel there was a huge upside to learning process documentation in the days when paper and pencil were the only tools available. When it comes to learning a process, *nothing* compares with the necessity of having to gather process information on the floor, in real time, using just your eyes and your brain—and writing it all down.

Back in the paper and pencil days, I not only developed elaborate notes, but often sketched exploded views of specific, more complex portions of the assembly. Also simple layouts, and other bits of information. I often *still* do these things.

Returning to the office, I would rewrite this information into a coherent, basic sequence of events. Using my new, consolidated and more formalized notes, I would return to the line for the process of "Layering-In" additional detail, which we will also talk about shortly.

Another, more fundamental reason for not relying solely on videotape requires me, to once again reference my days teaching sailing. We taught a class in celestial navigation; the age-old way of actually pulling out a sextant, taking sightings on three stars, and then calculating, and drawing three intersecting lines of position on a nautical chart. In those days the technology known as "Loran" was becoming popular; a technology which has now advanced to GPS. Our argument for taking the class was and is still valid—what if your battery goes dead? How do you know where you are, and perhaps more importantly where the rocks are?

I believe this principle to be valid here, as well. Learn the old-fashioned way first, *then*—when you are comfortable with your ability to do it in the fundamental way—you choose other tools and techniques which suit your personal style, I will have no argument.

— the Digital Camera

It may surprise you to know that I actually have reached the 21st century. My methodology, these days is a hybrid of old and new. While I still use paper and pencil to advantage, I supplement my notes with a digital camera. Modern cameras number images in sequence. By taking a photograph, or perhaps several photographs, of each major component part as it is added to the assembly I have an "in-sequence" record of the process. When the time comes to formalize my information, I can scroll through the photos and virtually write my basic sequence of events image by image, referencing my notes for verification and for details not captured in photographs.

As I've indicated I usually gather information on the floor in a rather informal manner, and then use my notes, photos, and memory of what I've seen—and yes, return visits to the shop floor—to formalize my documentation—again, in MS Excel. This methodology serves me in to important ways.

1. I can gather more information, more quickly by taking quick notes and photos than trying to be neat, precise, and complete on my first visit to the shop floor; a task I feel to be virtually impossible, anyway.
2. And most significantly I find the act of reviewing my data and writing out neat, precise, and complete documentation helps to fix the information in my mind. This proves quite useful when returning to the line to collect additional details, and yet again in the balancing process.

— Video

Using a video camera is an increasingly popular way to document work these days. And it is harder now to argue against video than in the times when cameras were heavy, bulky, and needed to be plugged in somewhere. But there are negatives to the sole use of video, and while must I accept its widespread usage, I will nonetheless voice my feelings here.

While you may be a great videographer, you *are* going to miss something. And you can't ask questions of the video, nor can you ask the video—after it is nestled in your hard drive—to show you that again from a different angle. You can look at the video as many times as you like, but it will only show you what was originally captured.

This doesn't mean that the vast majority of IE's who use video these days aren't successful, but there can be a danger in assuming that anything not shown on the tape is something that didn't occur. Regardless of how carefully detailed your analysis may be, you must still take your written documentation to the floor and carefully validate what you've observed and written against reality, and perhaps add a detail here and there.

Company Management and Unions are often in agreement about documenting all processes on video. Here I won't disagree, *but will suggest* that there can be unanticipated issues when using a single video, of a single person, at a single moment in time as the standard by which work is to be performed, and importantly, how long it takes.

Authors Note: I do need to stop here and emphasize the point that none *of the tools we've just been discussing—nor any new methods which you will devise for yourself—will preclude, or eliminate the need to go back to the floor and double check something now and then. As your documentation skills improve, unnecessary visits will be less frequent—and in a place like John Deere's Harvester plant, for example, where the main assembly line was a full third of a mile from our desks, I assure you that there is a lot of incentive to compile as much information as you can with each visit to the floor. So your skills will improve.*

But you will go back. It's an essential part of the process. The important thing is to not make unnecessary trips to learn something you should already know—But missed!

Collecting Information in Layers: Observation Cycles

By the time you set out to begin your actual documentation, in addition to the basic geography of the line, you should at this point have a fairly complete understanding of the product and its potential complexities. Our task now—one work station at a time—is to learn, understand, and to *record* the basic steps (elements) of the process. And *then* to seek out the details of how each of those elements are accomplished.

I'll repeat myself yet again – *I like to do that, so I do it often*—"A fundamental, *then* detailed understanding of an assembly process, as defined by its sequence of elements, is absolutely essential ...."

At this initial, *fundamental,* stage we don't care too much about the detail, the nuance, and the subtleties of method. Our purpose—for the moment—is to identify the major assembly steps which represent the overall work content of each station. Once we have established this basic sequence of events, with proper break points, we will then begin to look for, and add, those details which define and explain the work of each element. I like to refer to this as "collecting information in layers". First the basics, then with additional observations more and more detail until we have a complete documentation.

Work performed on an assembly is, by its very nature, a repetitive activity. To record that activity, we begin with what I call the first **Observation Cycle**. The first time through we're just going to watch for, and record, major events.

As you get more comfortable with this technique, you will begin to see more detail. If, while you are capturing the basic sequence of events, you happen to note further detail, *and can get it into your notes now, without missing part of what happens next*—do so. But again, our initial objective, at this point, is to capture the major elements and generate the basic sequence of events.

Below is an example of the initial, hand written notes for the first station of a hypothetical assembly line. The results of our first (or first few) observation cycle(s) may look something like Figure 1-5:

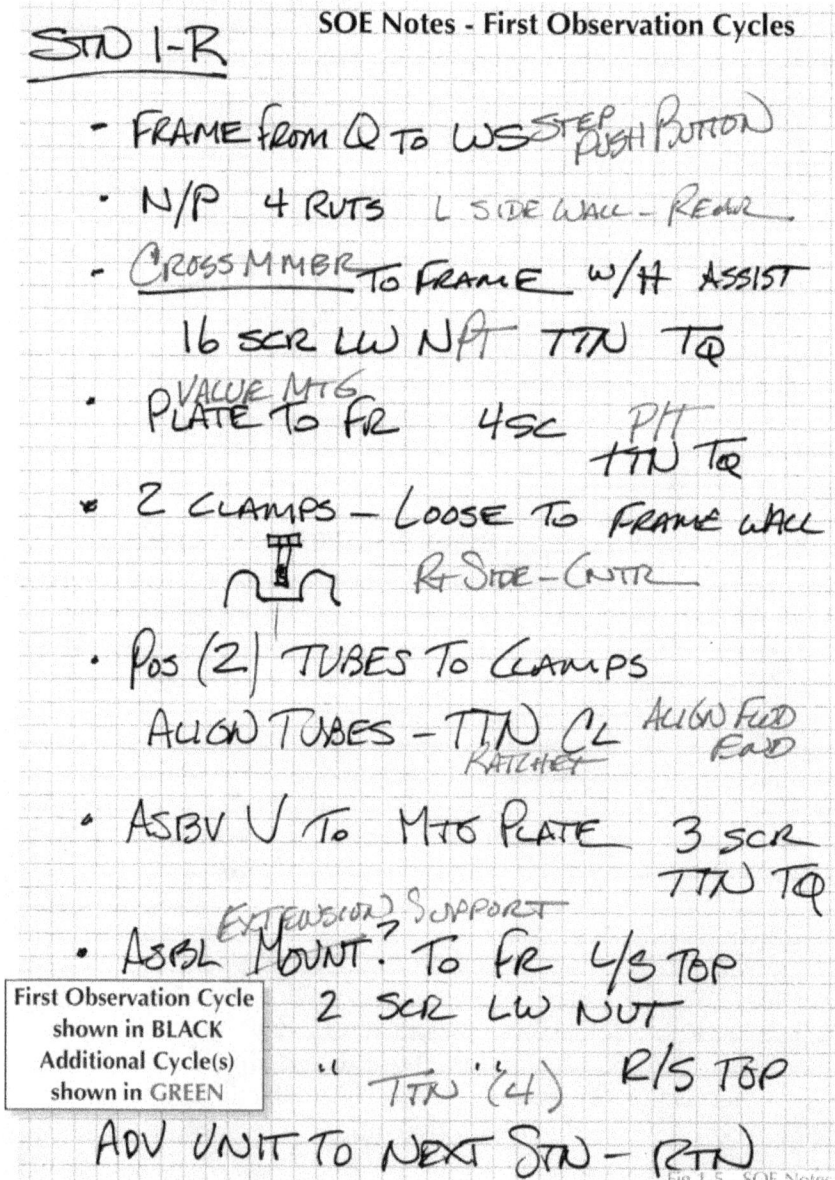

Fig 1-5 - SOE Notes

As you begin, don't be too concerned with the fact that *you are going to miss something*—even perhaps something major. Things are usually happening quickly and the first time through you're likely not to know what's going to happen next. So it's easy to be surprised by some activity you didn't expect, or don't yet understand, or to recognize (and name) some component, or to miss something while you are deciding what just happened—and busily writing it down. I say again, DON'T WORRY ABOUT IT. Just move on; keep up with the work that's occurring, and keep recording; *if you stop to make sense out of that last thing, you risk missing the next several activities.*

The nice thing about this methodology is that once the first cycle is over, you now actually have some documentation (in the form of the notes you have just taken) and a better understanding of the sequence. As the next cycle begins, you can now follow your notes and begin to anticipate what's going to happen next. Anything you see that's not in your notes is probably something you missed. And so you can "fill in the blanks" and complete the basic elemental sequence. Also, when you come to something you didn't understand the first time through, you are prepared to take a closer look, or perhaps—at an appropriate moment—ask a question.

This series of observation cycles may continue for as long as is necessary to capture the complete basic sequence. But you will be surprised—once you have *something* on paper—how quickly all of the rest becomes clear.

See, Capture, and Understand EVERYTHING

The ability to discern order from what appears to be chaos, and to efficiently and accurately capture and record work elements requires two skills—simple but very important—which I call **Recognition and Retention:**

— Recognition – The ability to see what you're looking at—and to understand what you have seen.

This is where being a quick study comes in quite handy. If you didn't already have what used to be known as "mechanical aptitude", you probably wouldn't be out there to begin with, so making sense of what you're seeing is well within the range of your capabilities. But, for most people doing it quickly *is* an acquired skill.

In the early 1970s, when I was a fledgling Industrial Engineer, I was also a part-time football referee—reaching the small college level by the time I moved to Milwaukee, and gave it up. Learning basic Industrial Engineering, studying and documenting work elements, and taking time studies, taught me to see – *really see* —what I was looking at. Serendipitously, this also proved extremely helpful to me as a football official.

At the same time, the speed of a football play, the fleeting occurrences, and the urgency to make the RIGHT decision, RIGHT now, quickly taught me things that were very helpful as a time study engineer. Principal among them was the ability see a play as it was—not what I expected to see, or what I *believed must have happened*—but what actually was, or had happened.

It is important—I would suggest vital—for the Industrial Engineer also to see, to recognize, and to acknowledge *only what was*. Not what was expected—or desired. If you start down this path you risk often *only* seeing what you expect, or (whether you are aware of it or not) *want* to see.

If you see something that you're not sure of, or that you don't understand, first of all —relax! You'll have another opportunity in the very next cycle to see what was missed. If, in the next or succeeding cycles, you're still not sure, expand your focus. See the activity in context of the overall work content of the station, or the line. Often some bit of work which makes no sense in isolation will suddenly become obvious when subsequent actions are observed.

— **Retention** – The ability to recall—after the fact—what you've seen.

Here the football analogy holds as well. I believe it possible to have, or to develop, the ability to retain images in your mind—to observe an event, and later not only recall it, but actually see it again in "your mind's eye". This ability is also a very useful skill when making notes on the line, and especially so when formalizing those notes later in the office.

A lot of people have the ability (perhaps learned in the lecture halls) to take reasonably neat, legible notes, and to do so fairly quickly. I do not! Even I am sometimes amazed at just how chaotic my own notes can be. The scribbles, abbreviations, and quick sketches can, and sometimes do, later prompt the question "what in the world did I mean by *that?*" The ability—aided of course by digital photographs –to see it again, in context, in my mind's eye usually provides the answer.

Authors Note: In my early days as an I.E., in an effort to keep up, I developed a system of abbreviations to quickly add information to my notes. Such things as "TTN" for Tighten (Hardware), "TQ" for Torque, "H" for w/Hoist, "w/A", for w/ Assist, and so on. Like workstation numbering systems, any set of abbreviations will do, as long as you understand them when later reviewing your notes.

Retaining process details is also helpful, as we will later see, in balancing the process—not only recalling linear sequence, but also limitations and dependencies of individual elements. The ability to visualize the process will inform you of what can be moved (and where), and what cannot.

Asking Questions

Asking questions is a necessary part of collecting, and recording, process information. There is an old saying that "people on the line know best how to build the product". This is at least partially true in the sense that the person doing the work has an intimate knowledge of the process, and its elements. The very things *you* are there to learn.

But to tap into that knowledge, it is important to ask questions in a way that does not interrupt the process as it occurs. Nothing can irritate—and possibly alienate,—an assembler working at an incentive pace than to stop and answer what might *at least be perceived* as an obvious, and perhaps foolish question. So the next important factor is to ask good questions.

In the first couple of observation cycles—when the most questions will occur to you—I would advise asking no questions at all. Sometimes questions answer themselves. A sub-assembly built early in the cycle, for example, may make no sense at all initially but may become perfectly obvious when a few moments later it is added to the unit.

If you think you have something figured out, but need confirmation, phrase the question as "is that for..." Or "did you do that because...?" If your perception was correct a simple yes answer is all that's required; and being right can sometimes enhance your credibility. If you are wrong, it will still convey the notion that you are thinking about what you are seeing, and may have simply seen something you have not previously encountered. Something that happens to everyone.

However you phrase your questions, don't interrupt an assembler who is obviously busy, or is at the moment concentrating on some task. Think first. Then at the appropriate time ask intelligent, concise questions which will provide you with the specific information you need. Again, each new cycle will add to your knowledge and understanding of the work sequence and can sometimes answer the question for you. Or if not, the additional information may aid you in asking better questions.

And always remember, sometimes what you *say* is not what is *heard* by the listener. Listen to your own question in your mind before speaking. The worst possible question is one *which can be heard as* "Duh, what's that for? I don't get it".

Occasionally pauses will occur in the workflow. These can be very good times for asking questions. A delay on the line may also provide the opportunity to connect with the assembler(s) on a human level, something we will talk more about in Part Two of this book, The Art of Work Measurement.

Using Video

Despite my earlier comments, there *are* advantages to using video. (Assuming, of course, that you have a video that shows you everything, or at least most of what you need to see). Foremost among the advantages is that as you observe you are not out on the line, in a noisy, possibly uncomfortable, or even hostile environment. Rather you are in a comfortable chair at your desk, probably with a cup of coffee close at hand.

With a video, you don't have to wait for the line to be running a specific model. You can watch at your own schedule, and are not interrupted by breaks, lunch time, or line stoppages. You can work at your own pace and, perhaps most importantly, you can stop, backup and take a second look. A downside, of course, is that you can't ask questions, and as I noted earlier, you only see what the video shows. So again, as I've mentioned previously, you *will* at some point have to hike on out there to the line.

When watching the video, if the cycle is not too long, forgo your notepad the first time through and just watch the activity. Then, following the same methodology is on-site observations, watch and take notes. On the first true observation cycle, when you begin taking notes, I recommend not stopping the video. Go through your initial note taking without pause, just as if you were on the line.

I have the belief that if you are forced to see something, in real time, as it is occurring—as with a sports referee, without benefit of instant replay—your ability to see what is happening is enhanced. Closely watching the video, the first time through without interruption focuses the attention and makes subsequent observations more productive.

After the first observation cycle is completed, and the fundamental sequences established in your notes, you are now free to take advantage of the opportunity to pause and/or replay individual activities as often as necessary. When you think you have it all, watch the tape one more time and just read along with your notes to verify the capture of every detail.

Later, when the notes are formalized, as we will discuss in the next section, it is vital—if at all possible—to take your documentation to the line and verify that the video has presented you a complete record of the work content. So whatever the reason; to verify, to ask questions, or to see for yourself something no clearly shown on the video, you *will* have to take that walk.

Author's Note: I once did a project from my office at home, where I was sent videos to analyze, document, and measure. The only opportunity to ask questions and verify was—what was then known as—a long-distance phone call, and a request for someone to go out and investigate on my behalf.

Taking Digital Photos

The introduction of the digital camera, has in my opinion, opened the doors to better, and easier, assembly line data collection. While I still take notes in the old-fashioned way I now document—in sequence—not only the assembly steps, but any other useful details, in easily reviewable digital photos.

There is, however, etiquette to taking photos of work as it is being performed on the shop floor. First, make sure that the person whose work is being photographed knows you are going to do so. You may notice that I said that "work is being photographed". Second, assure the assembler that you are only photographing the activity, not the person.

As with taking a video, if you are using a digital camera be sure the subject of your study knows you are doing so. Often, in the course of taking photographs of the work, the assemblers themselves appear in the photos. Many people don't really care, but some object strongly to having their picture taken—particularly by a stranger. Take care to explain to those people, with complete sincerity, that you have no need, and no desire, to take photographs of them.

You only care about the work, and the sequence of that work. If necessary, "trail along behind" and photograph parts after they've been installed, or sub-assembled, being sure the person is not in the frame. The important thing remains, you will have a photographic record, in sequence, of each activity.

No matter how well lit the line, you will almost certainly be using a flash. Always be aware of where you are pointing the camera in relation to the assembler. If—as occasionally happens—the assembler looks up at you just as you click the shutter, apologize and redouble your efforts not to have it happen again.

Lastly, but just as important, DON'T GET IN THE WAY! This is an admonition I make several times in these pages. But it is just that important. Whether taking notes, or photos, after a cycle or two, it's not too difficult to anticipate where the assembler is going to go next, so if necessary to get out of the way before they arrive. It's very easy to be caught up in the flow of the work, and your desire to get just the right angle, and yes, not to miss something. But it's embarrassing to say the least, to look up to see the assembler, with an exasperated look, standing there waiting for you to finish whatever you are doing, and MOVE!

4. Formalizing the Data

Process Information to Process Documentation

This brings us to a transition point; a simple, seamless, but nonetheless quite important shift, from collecting process information to creating process documentation.

When the basic sequence—and perhaps a few additional details—has been captured for one, or several, workstations it's now time to return to the office and begin to formalize what you know. Relying on notes, memory—and perhaps as in my case—a series of digital photos, begin to create the actual Sequence of Events. Again, in these post-modern times, I favor MS Excel for this purpose.

The reasons for stopping at this point to consolidate and formalize what you know should be somewhat obvious. Before you've gathered too much information to retain in memory—and before your notes are *too* full of information and begin to be indecipherable—it's time to sit down and make sense of it all.

For me, whether working from notes, or notes plus photographs, or video—and yes I do occasionally work from video if I can't avoid it—I find that, once again, the act of formally re-writing the process helps fix the details in my mind, something which is of great benefit in the next phase of the process. It also allows me to see each work station as not only a complete entity, but as a sum of its component elements.

When you have created the sequence of events in Excel, and entered everything which you know to this point, print this documentation and return to the line. You now have a "lead sheet" to follow, by which you can follow the work, searching out details. Again, you probably will not record *all* of the additional detail you want or need in just one more cycle, so continue the "layering in" process. With each observation cycle, as your knowledge of the process increases, the information gathering process becomes easier. You will find yourself anticipating events and capturing specific bits of information, allowing for a more specific and refined data capture with each cycle.

Depending on the length of the cycle, and the volume and complexity of the work within, it is likely to take several additional observation cycles before you are confident of having all of the information needed to transform your notes into a complete and accurate basic documentation. Within some limits, of course, the time it takes you to do this is much less important than the completeness and accuracy of your documentation.

When you feel that you have "gotten it all", it is time to return to the office and complete the sequence of events for the work station(s) which have been studied. Using your notes, photos, and perhaps video, to collect and gather what you know about the work content of each of the work stations you've observed. Updating your spreadsheet, transform this information into a more formal sequence of events. This may perhaps look something like Figure 1-6.

EI	Description	Mins
	Assembly Sequence of Events	
	Assembly Description: Medium Platform w/Extension Line No: B-17	
	Part No: KL-1003482-002 Analyst: TDS Date: 9/14/15	
1	Advance Frame from Queue to Work Station	
	Step, press Button and Return	
2	Attach Nameplate to Frame w/(4) Pop Rivits	
3	Loose Asbl Crossmember to Frame w/(16) Screws - w/Hoist	
	(4) Screws x (4) Places	
4	Tighten (16) Crossmember Screws w/Power Tool	
5	Torque (16) Crossmember Screws and Mark	
	w/Ratchet	
6	Assemble Control Valve Mtg Bracket to Frame w/(4) Screws - Power Tool	
7	Torque (4) Mtg Plate Screws and Mark	
	w/Ratchet	
8	Loose Asbl (2) Dbl Tube Clamps to R/S Inner Frame Wall	
9	Position (2) Hydr Tubes to Clamps on R/S Inner Frame Wall	
10	Align Tubes and Tighten (2) Clamps w/Power Tool	
	Align Tubes at fwd end	
11	Assemble Extension Cylinder Valve to Mtg Plate w/(3) Screws	
12	Tighten (3) Valve Mtg Screws w/Power Tool	
13	Assemble R/S Extension Support to Frame w/(2) Screws & Lock Nuts	
14	Assemble L/S Extension Support to Frame w/(2) Screws & Lock Nuts	
15	Tighten (4) Extension Support Screws w/Power Tool & Backup Wrench	
		Page 1 of 1

Fig 1-6 - Sample Seq of Events

It is now time to visit the line yet again. Using your now formalized and printed sequence of events, make additional observation cycles to again see what detail will further supplement the elemental information, and otherwise verify that the sequence is complete.

The final result is shown in figure 7. You will now use this additional information to update and complete the work content portion of the sequence of events.

	Assembly Sequence of Events		
Assembly Description: Medium Platform w/Extension		Line No: B-17	
Part No: KL-1003482-002	Analyst: TDS	Date: 9/14/15	

EI	Description	Mins
1	Advance Frame from Queue to Work Station *6 Steps to/fr* *Step, press Button and Return* *Unit travel int to steps*	
2	Attach Nameplate to Frame w/(4) Pop Rivits	
3	Loose Asbl Crossmember to Frame w/(16) Screws - w/Hoist *(4) Screws x (4) Places* *+ Flat Washers & Lock Washers*	
4	Tighten (16) Crossmember Screws w/Power Tool *Tighten Pattern*	
5	Torque (16) Crossmember Screws and Mark *w/Ratchet*	
6	Assemble Control Valve Mtg Bracket to Frame w/(4) Screws - Power Tool	
7	Torque (4) Mtg Plate Screws and Mark *w/Ratchet*	
8	Loose Asbl (2) Dbl Tube Clamps to R/S Inner Frame Wall	
9	Position (2) Hydr Tubes to Clamps on R/S Inner Frame Wall	
10	Align Tubes and Tighten (2) Clamps w/Power Tool *Align Tubes at fwd end* *Align Clamps for tightening*	
11	Assemble Extension Cylinder Valve to Mtg Plate w/(3) Screws *Orient Valve - Inlet Ports to rear of Unit*	
12	Tighten (3) Valve Mtg Screws w/Power Tool	
13	Assemble R/S Extension Support to Frame w/(2) Screws & Lock Nuts	
14	Assemble L/S Extension Support to Frame w/(2) Screws & Lock Nuts	
15	Tighten (4) Extension Support Screws w/Power Tool & Backup Wrench	
16	*Advance Unit to Station 2*	

Page __1__ of __1__

Fig. 7: Sample SOE w/Final Notes

Elemental times, as they are developed will be added to this documentation. Also discrete element by element parts and tools lists may be appended, as well.

Author's Note: I can only suggest—but I do so strongly—that even though you create the basic sequence of events, station by station—that you limit information to method steps until the entire sequence is complete. See the process in its entirety before generating elemental times, and adding parts lists and detailed tooling information.

Though we are documenting at an elemental level, it is important not to lose sight of the overall process of which each element is a part. Until the work content portion of the Sequence of Events is completed, you may sometimes make changes which may alter the requirements of material presentation, and equipment and tool set-up. Doing so after you've entered parts, and tools, and other information can often mean lot of extra work in revisions. Once again, capture the work content, in its entirety, before adding additional information.

Simultaneous, Partial-Simo, and Internal elements

It is possible, particularly if the sequence contains an element which represents an automated process, that a second element of work (or even more than one element) may be performed within the elapsed time of another. If the elapsed time for both are equal, these occurrences are be said to be **Simultaneous (or Simo)**, and only one of these times is included in the total work content.

More likely, one or the other element will have a longer duration and would thus be the "Controlling Element (or Time)", with the other, shorter, element(s) said to be **Internal** to the controlling time. Like the non-controlling element above, the time of the internal element is not added to the total work content.

It is also possible that work elements may overlap, in which case the elapsed time of the controlling element is added to the total work content. In addition, whatever portion of the overlapping element which falls *outside* of the parameters of the controlling element is included in the total work content. Such an occurrence is referred to as **Partial-Simo**.

Restrictions, Dependencies, and Balancers

In the linear sequence of an assembly process, there is a logical progression of work. A common term for this is that key process elements have inherently assigned priorities. Stated simply, some things *must* take place before others. When assembly processes are developed, priorities are generic. For example an Engine Cover would not *(because it could not)* be fitted to the unit before the Engine is in place. When the process is reorganized, and work assignments are changed to create a balance, it is vitally important to be aware of, and to know these priorities.

This is something we will discuss at greater length in Part Three of this book, but I believe it is valuable to be aware now, at the documentation stage, of these priorities and develop an understanding of what may later be moved, and to where, and perhaps most importantly, what may not.

Therefore, I want to simply introduce here the concepts which I call:

Restrictions – The introduction of (often) major component parts which are, by their nature, restricted to a particular place in the sequence, and are generally not (or cannot be) moved when balancing, or rebalancing.

Dependencies – Elements of work which are dependent on some other element of work already being performed (As an example, I refer again to the Engine Cover example, which cannot be installed until the Engine is in place. Its re-assignment is thus dependent on other element(s).

Balancers – A majority of work elements in the sequence will fall into one or the other of the previous categories. Some do not, and these—with some limitations— may be moved freely about the process. As such, these are the bits of work (and time) which I watch for, make note of, and later use to "fine tune" a balance.

Interaction Between Stations: Assisted Elements

Whether within a specific work area, or between adjoining work areas, or from one side of the line to the other, people (work stations) occasionally come together and work jointly to complete a single task. The work required to perform this task is assigned to *both* work stations. If an element, requiring two persons, takes a total of .500 minutes to accomplish, each person is assigned an appropriate work element of .500 minutes. The combination of these two elements adds 1.000 minute to the Total Work Content of the process.

For clarity, when documenting such occurrences, I believe it's necessary to adhere to the principle that "one person always controls". Both persons may be involved for the entire time, or commonly, one person will assist for a portion of the time. The key word here being 'assist".

In the sequences of events of *each* of these workstations, such a shared activity would be documented as follows:

> Station One:
>   Obtain Cylinder and position to Unit *w/Assist*   .500 Min
>
> Station Two:
>   *Assist* obtain Cylinder and position to Unit   .500 Min

Wherever any one person does something "with assist", there *must* be a matching element somewhere, performed by someone who does the "assisting". Occasionally, assistance is not required for the entire element. In this instance, time is allowed *only* for the actual assist.

For example:

> Station One Element:
> Obtain Hydr Cylinder w/Hoist and position to Unit <u>w/Assist</u>   .914 Min
>
> > *Obtain Hoist and connect to Cylinder w/Sling*   *.221 Min*
> > *Lift Cylinder and position above Unit*   *.218 Min*
> > *Lower and Position Cylinder to Unit w/Assist*   *.287 Min*
> > *Disconnect and aside Cylinder*   *.188 Min*

Station 2 Element:
<u>Assist</u> position Hydr Cylinder to Unit   .354 Min

Step to Unit   *.067 Min*
Assist Lower and Position Cylinder to Unit   *.287 Min*

Writing Conventions

Before concluding this discussion, I would be remiss not to spend a few minutes talking about the actual writing of process documentation. Along with a bit of discussion, I want offer the few simple rules for this by which I live. I know that I cannot enforce these rules, and I also know that some of you are going to think that some, at least, are quite silly.

But I have a very strong belief, reinforced by many years of observation of both writers (those working at the shop floor level) and readers (the Boss, or the Union, or whomever is going to review my work), that the more professional the writing is, the more it is going to be taken seriously, and given credibility as to the accuracy of the underlying work.

Author's Note: While I don't want to offend anyone, it seems to me that a lot of the things that we're going to talk about here; capitalizing part names, and others of the naming conventions that I will present—such as the arcane notion of correct spelling, or of even just making sense—are sometimes seen as outmoded habits which don't hold an important place in this post-modern world of brevity and instant communication. If you are one of these people, I'm sure that you believe this to be true, as do many of your peers.

I won't argue the point with you, but I would ask you to consider that formal process documentation created for the company for which you work, or perhaps for a client company, is not written for your peers, but almost certainly for people who hold the same archaic attitudes as mine.

A few simple rules:

Grammatically correct sentences are not required—but whole complete thoughts are.

Capitalize the start of each sentence (or thought) and use correct punctuation.

Capitalize items such as Part Names and Tool Names.

Abbreviations are OK, but they should be both understandable and *consistent*

For example, don't abbreviate assemble as ASBL in one part of your documentation and as ASSM in another.

Use numerical characters *(3)* rather than the word *(three)*—Put all numbers in parenthesis.

w/ is OK—and is I think actually preferable to the word "with".

For example, Asbl Plate to Frame w/(4) Screws.

If I were sending the following analysis to a friend on my phone, this might be acceptable:

> *get pump hsg and impeller cover from cont—place to bench*
>
> *get impeller—orient w sht shaft down and asbl into hsg*
>
> *apply locktite to hsg w brush—asbl gasket*
>
> *get impeller cover—asbl w lng shaft to pump w 4 screws*
>
> *tighten 4 cover screw w air tool*

If, on the other hand, I were offering this to my client, or to a union representative for critical review, or writing an instruction, etc, I might want to render it more like this:

> *Obtain Pump Housing and Impeller Cover from container and place to bench.*
>
> *Obtain Impeller—Orient with short Shaft down and assemble into Housing Flange.*
>
> *Apply Locktite to Housing w/Brush—Obtain Gasket and assemble to Housing.*
>
> *Obtain Impeller Cover and assemble over long Shaft to Pump w/(4) Screws.*
>
> *Tighten Impeller Cover Screws w/Air Tool.*

Part Two

The Art of Work Measurement

1. The Purpose of Work Measurement

Introduction

This book is not about how to measure work. Consequently, what is offered here is not an instruction on using the various tools available. There are plenty of books on the taking of time studies, and most, if not all predetermined time systems have instructions, and/or application rules for their data sets. Similarly, new age work measurement software systems provide, or will sell to you, excellent training programs.

Rather, much of what will be discussed herein is what I call the "art" of work measurement. Yes, we *will* review the various work measurement methodologies; principally time study and standard data. But I want to instead emphasize the interpersonal skills, and philosophical and behavioral approach necessary to make on-the-floor application of these tools easier, less hostile, and more productive.

In manufacturing, the days of individual, one-to-one incentive (or piece-work) pay systems are mostly gone[1]. However, "group incentives" and "pay plans" are quite commonly applied to modern-day assembly-line operations. In such a plan, pay for each associate in the group is collectively determined by the *group's* performance against an overall standard. A standard derived from the total work content (measured as time) of the unit being produced. So it is quite likely that the person you study, and measure, today will ultimately be paid based upon the times you calculate and apply to the individual work elements. And each and every person you study will know it!

So the relationship which you establish, however briefly, with the people you study can have an impact on the success of your work measurement activities and—most importantly—in establishing work standards which are fair to all.

Why Do We Measure Work?

Given how much of a bother, and a challenge it is, and how much animosity has and can sometimes still be created, the question must be asked "Why do we measure work?"

Every specific answer to this question is, in fact, part of a larger, and very simple, all-encompassing reason. Virtually no business, and certainly no manufacturing operation, can function efficiently without knowing—to some level of accuracy—just how long it takes to do things. There are a nearly infinite number of "How Long" questions which must be answered. Not only *"How long does it take to make that widget?"*, but *"How long does it take to set up the Widget machine?* Or *"How long does it take to get that very important widget to the assembly line?"* or *"How long does it take to get the finished product into a box*

---

[1] Although re-energized versions of this method of incentive pay seem to be gaining ground in the areas of distribution center order picking, and similar activities.

and onto a truck? and so on." The answer to very nearly all of the many questions is often "I don't know, let's take a study and find out".

On the assembly line itself the simple and obvious truth is that to organize a line, and staff it with the required number of people to meet demand, we must know how long it takes to assemble (and perhaps to test and/or package) one complete unit. To balance the often very many work elements amongst the sometimes many work stations into an efficient, synchronous work flow it is necessary to know how much time is required for each individual task.

A corollary to "How Long" is the question "When". It is amazing to think about how many times in a manufacturing operation *that* question must be answered. If we are building Lawn Mowers for example, we must supply, among many other parts, Mower Blades to the appropriate work station. "When?" should we do this, you ask. The perfect answer to that question—in this just-in-time world—is that a new Blade be supplied, just as the previous mower is completed and sent on its way.

This perfect, one-to-one delivery of parts may be difficult, if not impossible to maintain, and the determination must be made as to how many Blades must be present at any given time, and *when* they are to be delivered. To assure that an efficient, adequate supply of parts is available to each station we need to measure the time it takes to make (or to unpack) and to deliver appropriate numbers of each part to the right place on a timely basis. Using our Mower Blade again as an example, working back from when blades are needed at the assembly line defines when to start setting up the machine, and when to start making Blades. This also requires knowing, to some degree, times required not only for each step in the in-plant process, but each element of the supply chain which delivers the material from which Blades are produced. Tasks which have kept engineers occupied since the days of Henry Ford.

These many bits of time information help answer many additional business questions, as well. Knowing production times allows for accurate scheduling, completion dates, and on-time delivery. More germane to our discussion here, how long it takes to build a complete assembly, factored by demand—how many of those assemblies must be produced in a given time—provides the answer to how many people are needed on the line.

2. The Tools of Work Measurement

The Sequence of Events (Again??)

Being somewhat Old School, I have said many times that work measurement is the heart of Industrial Engineering. And so I hear you ask, "If this is true why have we been spending so much time on something else—process documentation, in the form of the sequence of events?" I say this because the concept of the sequence of events is the very heart of work measurement.

To be accurately measured, the work content of a task is broken down into individual elements. And to each element is applied a discreet time value. To calculate that time value, the work content of each element, with a few exceptions, must be analyzed and identified—as a Sequence of Events—and then timed by one of the methodologies available for that purpose.

Author's Note: Exceptions to this would be, for example, an element representing only process time, or a small element which may be measured in its entirety with a single time, or single line of analysis.

Work Measurement Methodologies

Work may be measured in three principle ways:

1) The "Estimate"—A method which may, at times, be useful—based upon circumstance, as well as the experience, and ability of the estimator. But can very possibly prove to be wildly inaccurate, as well.

2) "Snap-Back Time Study"—Which can be *very* accurate—or sometimes not (depending on a combination of the skill of the analyst and the cooperation of the subject).

3) The application of "Standard Data"—Which can also be very accurate—depending on use of the appropriate level of data, the accuracy of the data itself, and again, applicator skill and circumstance.

There are actually additional work measurement methodologies—the most notable among them being "Continuous Watch Time Study", and "Work Sampling". But since these are generally impractical for the development of elemental times, they will not be included in this discussion.

So, as promised, we will take a brief look at the two *viable* methodologies mentioned above.

Snapback (or Three-Watch) Time Study

Snapback Time Study has fallen out of favor in recent times, partly because it is perceived (accurately so) to be sometimes difficult to do. And also because "new age" analysts increasingly favor technological solutions to difficult tasks.

The genesis of the name three-watch, or snapback, comes from the literal fact that in earlier days, time study boards carried three stopwatches, and a hand lever with linkage which would activate all three watches at the same time. Watches would be pre-set so that, at the push of the lever, one watch would begin timing the current element being observed, one watch would stop, showing the elapsed time of the previous element, and one watch would reset to zero—to await the next element to be observed.

Time Study Worksheet	PART NO		DESC												
DATE	DEPT		WORK CENTER					SUPERVISOR							
OBSERVER			OPERATOR							OPER NO					
START TIME			STOP TIME					ELAPSED TIME							
OPERATION, READINGS AND COMPUTATIONS															
ELEMENT DESCRIPTION			READINGS										TOTAL ALLOWED MINS	NO OF OBSV	AVG MINS	PERF %	NORMAL ELEM MINS
			1	2	3	4	5	6	7	8	9	10					
REMARKS										TOTAL MINS					
										PF & D ALLOWANCE _____ %					
APPROVED (Signature)			DATE					STANDARD PER UNIT _____		STD MINS STD HOURS					
Form: TS-1996										PAGE _____ OF _____ PAGE(S)					

Fig 2-1 - Time Study Form

The Time Study Form (Fig 2-1) is an example of such forms on which observed times are recorded, and work standards may be calculated. The form provides rows for each work element (*the Sequence of Events*) to be observed and timed. Each elemental row contains a series of boxes (usually 10) in which observed times are recorded. Pressing the time study board's lever starts one watch to begin timing the first element. At the breakpoint, at which that element ends, the lever is pressed, stopping the first watch and starting the next to begin timing the next element. At the same time the third watch is reset to zero.

The elapsed time of the first element (first watch) is then read and recorded to the first box of row one. This sequence is repeated down the list of elements until the work cycle is completed. When the last element has been timed, the sequence continues with column two, and so on until an adequate number of work cycles have been observed and timed.

Following the "Observed Time" boxes of each elemental row, are additional data boxes, as follows:

(Total Allowed Time) The sum of all *allowed* observed times for that element.

(No of Observations) The total number of allowed observations for that element.

(Average Elem Mins) The sum of allowed elemental times, divided by the number of allowed observations.

(Perf %) An overall Performance Rating for the allowed observations of that element—determined by the analyst—and entered as a percentage.

(Normal Elem Time) Average time is factored by the performance rating percentage. The resulting time value—the average, normalized time—is recorded in this final elemental box.

The information and calculations above are entered for each elemental row. Normal Elemental Times for each row are totaled, and entered at the bottom of the form. This number represents the final result of the study—"Overall Allowed Elemental Time". It is this time which is applied to the corresponding element in the process sequence of events. Applying a time to all elements of the sequence of events generates a very significant and useful number—the "Total Work Content" of the assembly process.

Authors Note: Or, in the case of a "Stand-Alone" study, intended to generate a work standard for a single activity, the sum of elemental time would be factored by the appropriate allowances (Personal, Fatigue, and Delay—usually referred to as "PF&D") to create the standard. For a work group, such as an assembly line, PF&D allowances are applied, at a later time, to the sum of all elemental times—Total Work Content (TWC) to generate the "Group Standard".

Dis-Allowed Observations

A powerful feature of snapback (or, in fact any) time study—contributing greatly to the overall accuracy—is the ability to "disallow" and thus exclude observations whose activities fall outside the prescribed method. Such exclusions may be for a variety of reasons;—a fumble, or a drop, or an interruption, or pause, or even a temporary deviation in work pace, setting this observation apart from the others, and therefore outside the boundaries of the performance rating.

Times for such anomalous elements are recorded as usual, but are then circled and appended with a brief notation as to the reason for the exclusion. Like many of my old-time colleagues, I developed some shorthand codes for identifying the various occurrences which may disqualify an observation. Additionally, this supplemental information provided by these notations, often proves helpful when compiling a study, rating performance, or in defending a challenged work standard.

Authors Note: For example: D = Drop, F = Fumble, H = Hesitation or Pause, EX = Extra Motions, and so forth. Any system of codes will do, as long as they are somewhat understandable (or explainable), and are used with consistency. Once you establish and begin to use these codes—Stick with them.

Such anomalies fall into one of two categories. Human beings are not automatons, and random anomalies, and workplace interruptions which are outside the control of the associate are likely to occur. These should be, and are, included in the work standard. These legitimate occurrences are recognized as **Unavoidable Delays**, and are compensated for as the "D" in the PF and D allowances[2] which are applied as the final standard is calculated. Therefore, these random, yet legitimate, occurrences must be removed from the average minutes calculation to avoid being compensated for a second time.

Other occurrences are considered to be within the control of the associate performing the work. These are recognized as **Avoidable Delays**, and are not, and should not be, compensated for in the work standard. Such things as fumbles, drops, pauses, hesitations, extra (unnecessary) motions which are outside the prescribed method, temporary (and excessive) changes in work pace, which will fall outside the parameters of the assigned performance rating, and other like events are also noted and excluded from the "allowed time" summation, and are not included in the allowance add-on.

Performance Rating (for Time Study)

In addition to uncorrupted average times, a significant factor in the accuracy of all time studies—snapback or continuous watch—is the performance rating of observations.

While observing work activity and recording observed times, and "circling out" disallowed times when necessary, the analyst must also determine the pace at which the subject is working. Determining an accurate, representative work pace for each elemental average time can be challenging but at the same time, vitally important. The applied performance rating percentages literally determine the final normalized time for each element, and thus for the entire study.

The first and most important aspect of performance rating is also perhaps the most misunderstood and abused—performance *rating is a measure of work pace, not of method.* Observed work is either performed within the acceptable, and pre-agreed-upon, parameters of the prescribed method, or it is not. If not, the observation is excluded, as discussed above. If the work is performed as expected, the method plays no part in determining the pace, or speed with which the work is being performed. Thus, work pace and the resulting performance rating is wholly a measure of *speed*, or sometimes lack of speed.

Normalizing Observed Times

The term "normalized", as applied to time study, is derived from the act of adjusting an average *observed time* to represent a "normal" pace—the time to be expected of an "average associate" working at a 100% pace. Observations which are determined to be at 100% are used—un-adjusted—in the calculation of an elemental time, or of a work standard. However, when it is determined that the timed work element was performed at a *faster* than normal (100%) pace, the

---

[2] PF and D (Personal, Fatigue, and Delay) Mutually agreed-upon percentages—usually a part of the labor agreement.

resulting time must be factored UP to represent a 100% pace, thus "normalizing" the time. For example:

Avg Observed Time for an Element: .287 Minutes

Work Pace (Performance Rating) is determined to be : 110%

.287 x 1.10 = .315 **Avg Normal** Elemental Minutes

On the other hand, when it is determined that the timed work element was performed at a *slower* than normal (100%) pace, the time must be factored DOWN to normal:

Avg Observed Time for an Element: .287 Minutes

Work Pace (Performance Rating) is determined to be : 90%

.287 x .90 = .268 **Avg Normal** Elemental Minutes

Fig 2-3 demonstrates a typical completed Snap-Back Time Study.

Time Study Worksheet		PART NO		DESC	Asbl Nameplate to Frame w/(4) Rivets			
DATE 9/03/15	DEPT A480		WORK CENTER Line 22-B			SUPERVISOR Jacoby		
OBSERVER Tom Shropshire			OPERATOR Ed Fletcher				OPER NO 1304	
START TIME 12:47 pm		STOP TIME 12:54 pm			ELAPSED TIME 6.58 Min			

OPERATION, READINGS AND COMPUTATIONS

	ELEMENT DESCRIPTION	READINGS										TOTAL ALLOWED MINS	NO OF OBSV	AVG MINS	PERF %	NORMAL ELEM MINS
		1	2	3	4	5	6	7	8	9	10					
1	Obtain N/P and Rivet Gun - pos Rivet to (1) N/P hole	.09	.10	.10	.08	.09	.11	.10	.10	.09	.10	.990	10	.099	110	.1089
2	Position N/P and Rivet to 1st Frame Hole - Pull Trigger	.12	.11	.12	.11	.13	.12	.13	.11	.12	.12	1.119	10	.112	110	.1232
3	Load Rivet to Gun for Next N/P Hole	.05	.06	.06	.05	.05	(.11) F	.06	.05	.06	.07	.510	9	.057	110	.0623
4	Align N/P, a/r - Position Rivet to 2nd Hole - Pull Trigger	.10	.08	.09	.10	.09	.09	.08	.11	.09	.10	.930	10	.093	105	.0977
5	Load Rivet to Gun for Next N/P Hole	.07	.05	.06	.06	.06	.07	.06	.06	.06	.07	.610	10	.062	100	.0620
5	Position Rivet to 3rd Hole - Pull Trigger	.07	.06	.07	.07	.06	.07	.08	.07	(.12) H	.08	.630	9	.070	105	.0735
6	Load Rivet to Gun for Next N/P Hole	(.13) D	.06	.06	.07	.06	.07	(.10) F	.06	.06	.06	.500	8	.050	100	.0625
7	Position Rivet to 3rd Hole - Pull Trigger	.08	.06	.07	.07	.06	.07	.08	.07	.07	.07	.700	10	.070	105	.0735
8	Load Rivet to Gun for Unit - Aside Rivet Gun	.05	.06	.06	.06	.06	.07	.06	.06	.06	.06	.590	10	.059	105	.0619

REMARKS		
F = Fumble, H = Hesitation, D = Drop	TOTAL MINS	.7255
	PF & D ALLOWANCE ——— %	
APPROVED (Signature) Ray Massey DATE 9/07/15	STD HOURS PER UNIT	STD MINS

Form: TS-1996

Fig 2-2 - Sample Time Study

PAGE 1 OF 1 PAGE(S)

Despite being one of the keys to fair and accurate study results, I have found that the perceived subjective nature of the performance rating can make it the most challenged aspect of a disputed time study. And often the hardest to defend. So, the credibility of the analyst is of great importance. Performance Rating is a skill—both learned and practiced. For that reason, adequate training in "seeing" work pace objectively, and for what it is, is essential.

Authors Note: In the now long-ago days when time study was a common and almost universally applied work measurement tool, Industrial Engineering departments would routinely schedule weekly meetings to watch and rate filmed activities performed at various paces, so as to hone their ability to recognize a "normal" pace —and variations from it. And to assure being "in sync" with others in the department.

Newer Time Study Tools

As time, and technology progressed, digital time study boards started replacing the venerable stopwatches. While the printed forms, and the method of recording times and calculating work standards remained the same, digital boards featured a single readout, and buttons for start, stop, and reset.

To begin the study, pushing the "start" button begins the timing of the first element —the running time is displayed. Pushing the start button at the elemental break point both stops (and remembers) timing the first element and begins timing the next. Holding the button down would freeze and display the elapsed time of the element just concluded. When the button was released, running time of the new current element was displayed, and so on... This innovation provided a significant increase in ease, and efficiency in the taking of a time study.

The age of computers (and software applications) brought forth the handheld devices, in which study elements could be preloaded and displayed as boxes on the screen. Touching an on-screen box with a stylus would begin timing that element. Timing would continue until the same, or another box, was touched, beginning the next observation while placing the previous time into memory. On completion of the study, this automatically tabulated data would be stored, and downloaded later to a PC.

There were attractive features to using these devices; principally the ability to isolate, observe and time elements of a much shorter duration. This was desirable in settings where elements were short, and often performed very quickly. (For example, at a distribution center—the need to scan large numbers of differing items —often performed at an incentive pace—one at a time.

However, in an industrial setting, I feel there are significant limitations in taking time studies this way. Some years ago, when I was briefly exposed to this method of time study, the entry of performance rating was not possible. But the biggest limitation, I felt, was the inability to "circle out" and exclude elemental anomalies, as can be done with time study form and a pencil. This forced the acceptance of all observations—method pure or not—and led to the taking of hundreds, sometimes thousands of observations in an effort to "water down" the effect of flawed observed times so as to achieve an "acceptable" level of accuracy.

Standard Data: Facts and Misconceptions

The other viable option for setting work standards, or for generating times for elements of work, is the somewhat newer, but certainly time-tested and proven technique of applying Standard Data. "Standard Data" is the commonly applied term for the more descriptive, but somewhat windy phrase, "Pre-Determined Time Systems".

I have found that as non-industrial engineers (manufacturing engineers, process engineers, and practitioners of various Lean methodologies) become increasingly involved in work measurement activities, a couple of things are happening, more or less simultaneously. One, traditional time study is being mostly ignored in favor of timing techniques which are easier to apply, but are of sometimes dubious accuracy. And two, Standard Data—the true bedrock of modern-day work measurement—is generally misunderstood, and is often dismissed for a variety of mostly invalid reasons.

The first misconception to address is the notion that "Pre-Determined Time Systems" and Standard Data are two different things. They are NOT! It must be understood that the terms "Pre-Determined Time System" (or PDTS) and "Standard Data" are synonymous. The confusion comes, I believe, in the way that IEs commonly use these terms.

While they both mean the same thing (a PDTS is Standard Data and Standard Data is a PDTS), the terms are often used to describe two different types, or "levels" of data. Pre-determined Time System usually refers to standard data at its lowest levels. Measurement systems such as MTM, or M.O.S.T., or MSD (Master Standard Data), and several other such tools are considered to be either first level, or lower level data. These represent time application tools which are developed, and along with adequate training programs and certifications, are commercially available.

What is generally called Standard Data, on the other hand, are systems of what I call "Data Sets", including appropriate Applicator Instructions. Such data systems are created using lower level data, or sometimes time study or other method. The elements of this "higher level" data represent not single motions, but whole tasks, and are used to apply work standards in a specific area, such as Turret Lathe Set-Up, or General Assembly, or Paint Line (Hanging and Unloading), and, well, virtually anything.

Higher level data systems may be included in a broader "Management" software package, but are most often developed locally to provide easy to use, and relatively quick to apply data for use by a given company or department, and statistically proven to be acceptably accurate, within the context of their intended use.

Standard Data: Application

In practice the application—the actual generation of time values—of standard data is generally simpler than the taking of a time study, and much less subjective.

First, the work to be measured is defined as (you know) a sequence of events. Depending on the nature of the task, its elemental scope, as well as the system being employed, and the level of data used, elements of the analysis itself may be refined as a series of single motions, such as in the MTM analysis we saw in Part One; obtaining a Pencil, placing it to a Tray, and sliding the Tray aside.

1		Obtain Pencil from Desktop and Place to Tray			28.2
	a.	Reach 13" to Pencil	R-HA-13"	8.9	
	b.	Grasp Pencil w/Thumb and (2) Fingers	G-1A	2.0	
	c.	Move Pencil 8" to Tray	M-A-8"	9.7	
	d.	Position Pencil to center section of Tray	P-1S	5.6	
	e.	Release Pencil	V1-1	2.0	
2		Slide Tray to Rear of Desktop			34.9
	a.	Reach 4" to edge of Tray	R-HA-4"	4.9	
	b.	Contact Tray w/Hand	G-5	0.0	
	c.	Slide Tray w/Hand 16" to rear of Desktop	M-B-16"	15.8	
	d.	Release Tray	V1-2	0.0	
	e.	Return Hand to starting position - 18"	R-HA-18"	14.2	
Fig 2-3 - MTM Analysis		**Total TMU:**			**63.1**

Or, if the sequence of events contains elements of a broader scope, representing sometimes many individual motions, higher level data may well be a better choice. Again, in the work element analysis, component element(s) are described in the SOE, and to each is applied one, or more, "higher level" data element(s). Examples of such higher level data elements might be:

Tighten First Screw w/Power Tool

Which would include obtaining the tool, moving to the fastener, positioning and activating the tool, tighten time, and asiding the tool.

Tighten Each Additional Screw w/Power Tool

Including moving to the next fastener, positioning and activating the tool, and tighten time. No obtain or aside of the tool is included.

So the analysis for the work element "Tighten (4) Screws with Power Tool" might look like this:

1. Tighten First Screw w/Power Tool (TFP-01) .278 Freq = 1 .278
2. Steps to Obtain/Aside Tool (4 Steps) (WE-04) .278 Freq = 1 .037
3. Tighten Each Additional Screw w/Power Tool (TFP-A) .121 Freq = 3 .363
Total Work Element Time: .678 Min

Author's Note: Any steps between fasteners may be included in the Tool Use element. But more likely, such a variable would need to be added as a separate element. The applicator instructions would explain.

Sometimes a work element analysis may consist of a single element of data, such as:

Load Small Part to Fixture with (1) Toggle Clamp

Which would include obtaining a Small Part (as defined in the Application Instructions) and positioning it into a Fixture and tightening (1) Toggle Clamp.

Author's Note: Other elements within the Data Set might provide for such variations as multiple Clamps, or different type(s) of Clamps.

Whether using "Low Level" data or "Higher Level" data sets, the theory of application is the same. First define the elements of the analysis. Then, element by element, choose the appropriate time value from a chart, or list and apply that elemental time, (and its identifying code number) to that line item.

"Armchair Standards"

Another misconception, often leading to unfair criticism or outright dismissal of standard data, is the notion that an engineer can just sit back in the office, pick a few data elements and create a work standard—without ever going to the floor and seeing "reality". Thus creating what is derisively referred to as an "Armchair Standard". In fact, nothing could be further from the truth.

As I hope I have conveyed earlier, proper preparation (in the form of elemental documentation) must precede the establishment of time values for most, if not all of the required work elements. It is certainly necessary before performing a time study, and I would argue that this investigation—and thorough documentation—is, if anything, more important prior to the application of standard data.

There are however, exceptions. Some years ago, I was contracted to create a standard data application system for establishing work standards in the "finishing area" of a large foundry which produced castings of small engine parts, and other like items. The intent of the project was in fact to create standard data from which could be applied work standards, simply by reviewing part characteristics from the engineering drawing, and then applying appropriate data elements.

Each data set, depending on the type of casting,—contained, first of all, a "constant" element; which would be applicable to cover all basic work common to all parts of that particular type. Additional data sets for each part type, were included to cover all the variable work elements which might be required to "finish" a given type of casting, and thus prepare it for machining.

For example, "Grind off Parting Line" on a circular or round casting, would include a selection of elements for differing part weights and sizes, and arcs of grind. This data—which *could* be applied merely by reviewing part drawings—meets the understood definition of the term "Armchair Standard". For the occasional circumstance where the data did not cover the work in its entirety, a trip to the shop floor was indeed necessary to obtain additional information, or perhaps to measure some element in a more traditional way.

The data, including comprehensive application instructions, was validated for completeness and accuracy, and accepted by the union industrial engineer. Standards, in this limited and very specific context, require a thorough knowledge of the work area at large, a complete understanding of the data, and even then, the occasional visit to the shop floor.

While not uncommon, this type of "armchair" data application is certainly not the norm. So, I say yet again, expect to perform a complete and proper preparation before turning to the task of work measurement.

A Final Word

The subjective nature of performance rating in time study has been previously noted. This may sometimes lead to disagreements, and challenges which can be difficult to defend. But with the application of standard data, no such situation exists. Like time studies, standards generated with data are reviewed, and often gone over "with a fine tooth comb" by union representatives trained in the data system used. The time value applied to each element is either correct—or it is not. If a data element is found to be misapplied, it is easily corrected. But there is also a danger in the use of Standard Data—one which, I believe, requires emphasis.

Snapback Time Study inherently provides for the capture of all work performed. In the repetitive timing of complete work cycles, everything which occurs between the various breakpoints is automatically included. In fact, as we have discussed, it is important to note and *exclude* anomalous elemental observations.

With the application of standard data, however, time is applied to work elements, as listed in the sequence of events, and within the various elemental analyses. It is therefore always possible to miss—and thus inadvertently exclude—some action which may very probably impact the final time value.

So I'm going to repeat a portion of a phrase from an earlier part of this book. *"See, and capture, (and measure) everything"*. This is the Number One priority. It may sound like heresy, but in my opinion it is more important to account for every bit of necessary work—and to incorrectly apply *some amount* of time to it—than it is to get a perfectly accurate time on every element on the list, only to have discovered, upon review, that something is just not there. If an omission goes un-noticed, your standard is probably wrong, to some degree. If it is discovered, you risk appearing to be inattentive to your work—or worse.

3. The Philosophy of Work Measurement

Introduction: "Fair, Correct, and Complete"

The goal of work measurement can be to create a discreet work standard, or as we have been discussing, to apply a time value to an element of work as part of a larger standard, or as an element of data. But whatever the immediate goal, the purpose of the activity is to calculate, and to apply a performance expectation which others are expected to achieve. This, for me, is the genesis of the expanded term I will use here; the "Fair, Correct, and Complete Standard". And I want to spend a few minutes discussing those things which I feel are necessary to achieve this goal.

A Fair Standard

First, a Fair Analysis. In any group of Industrial Engineers, I am hoping that talk of fairness is preaching to the choir. That said, I will offer a few thoughts of my own.

1.   Fairness *should* be automatic, but is sometimes not. Looking back, I have known Industrial Engineers—not many but a few—who just wrote tight standards, and who relished finding ways to reduce existing standards. I like to believe that there are far fewer of those kinds of people in the profession today than there were in the past.
2.   Some Industrial Engineers (perhaps many of us, at one time or another) may lose objectivity. Sometimes you're just having a bad day. Sometimes the subject of the study is extremely belligerent (and you just don't want to give anything away to *that* guy).
3.   And sometimes—it must be said—the work measurement analyst may lack the requisite skills. This is not uncommon, but is usually soon corrected with time, experience—and possibly a couple of painful standard reviews. Ours is, after all, very much a skill learned by doing. No amount of study and/or classroom exercise can equal actually being out on the floor facing the challenges of real world work measurement.

So, I think it's fair to suggest that all of us who, at one time or another, reach conclusions which affect the lives of others, should stay conscious of our obligation to do so fairly.

And fairness is of course a two-way street. Whether a direct employee, or a contractor or consultant, hired to do a specific project, you are being paid to generate elemental times and standards which are accurate and fair to *everyone*. Just as fairness to the employee is important, fairness to the employer or to the client is equally our goal. And again, business decisions need (or should be) based on what is, not what *anyone* wants it to be.

There is no benefit to be had from an incorrect standard; either way. Especially to the creator of the standard, for a bad work standard, *left uncorrected* will sooner or later will make you look—in the eyes of your employer, or to those who must work to that standard, or often both—like a jerk.

A Complete and Correct Standard

And to be Fair, a work standard must be two things; Correct and Complete.

As to being Correct, I'm speaking of correct *Elemental Times*. Work measurement is a "bottom up" activity. Elements, from the lowest levels are combined into larger work elements, and sometimes combined yet again to ultimately form a work standard. So it is axiomatic to say that "if the elements are correct (and correctly timed or applied) the standard is correct".

So, the last factor in the equation is, you guessed it, the standard must be Complete. Combined elements—again, at any level—must each represent a complete analysis. Whether using a stop watch, or applying data, the analysis (yes, the sequence of events) must contain and account for *every* bit of work necessary to fully accomplish the task being measured.

4. The Art of Work Measurement

Introduction

As a technical exercise, work measurement is a sometimes complex and challenging, but essentially straightforward activity. However, regardless of the methodology, there is almost always human contact involved. And very often that contact is with someone who doesn't really want to have to deal with you, and is skeptical—to say the least—of whatever conclusions you may draw. And that's just the information gathering, or documentation phase. Showing up with a stopwatch takes things to yet another level.

So work measurement is *more* than just a technical exercise. I know some of my former colleagues will scoff at the notion, but my firm belief is that true, well performed, work measurement at least ventures into the territory of being an art form. Even the actual application of data, usually done away from the shop floor, requires the skilled, and sometimes imaginative, use of data sets to craft that "fair, correct, and complete" work standard, so desired by everyone. And becoming skillful in this art, as I have previously suggested, requires appropriate training and experience—which may be gained, ironically, only by doing the work without initial benefit of said experience.

Gaining Acceptance

The remainder of this section will focus on interactions with individuals, and sometimes groups, on the shop floor, whose cooperation is not always assured.

In virtually any group there is the possibility of encountering one or more study subjects who view the company management—often in terms of pay and benefits—as an adversary. In practical terms, the nameless, faceless, adversaries of the "front-office" are something of an abstraction. You, on the other hand, are the real-world representative of that abstraction, and you are right there to see, and to interact with.

A somewhat subjective, but vitally important, aspect of your relationship with those whom you would analyze, or study to generate elemental time values, and ultimately work standards, is the skill, or technique, (or, as I insist, art) which is of great, but underappreciated, value to the Industrial Engineer. That technique is to **Gain Acceptance**.

By this I'm speaking of acceptance of the study—and of course the person taking the study—by the members of the work group, or department who are the subjects of your efforts; and in particular, the person whom you are studying at that moment. Here many may use the term "Buy-In". Engage the operator, explain your purpose and gain their trust and cooperation. Once you have done so, the study will go, pardon the pun, like clockwork. However, this is not always possible.

Way back in the days when individual piece-work rates were common, and when the relationship between the person setting a work standard, and the person whose pay would be based upon that standard, was so much more serious, I adopted a philosophy which accepted that—human nature being what it is—even when the relationship was amiable—the person being studied was obligated by self-interest to try and fool me somehow into writing a looser standard. I learned not to resent this; it was simply my job, as a work measurement professional, not to be fooled.

Even in these more enlightened times, given the infinitely variable nature of people and circumstance—and the inherent mistrust of "the guy with the stopwatch"—I do not believe that complete cooperation is always possible. The goal, yes, is to create that brief partnership where you work *with* the operator to produce a correct, complete, and fair standard. But, if I must, I'll settle for acceptance.

As I have indicated, every department, or cell, or workgroup will have it least one person who wants nothing to do with you, and will mistrust everything you say and do. That same group, however, will almost certainly have at least one person who is friendly, willing to find common ground, and to cooperate with your goal—that being a fair standard. I may not study that person first, but that *is* the principle person of whom I will ask questions, and offer explanations as to my purpose. Rest assured everything said to that person will soon be known by everyone in the group, and others will come around.

Being a Person

A lot has been said and written about the techniques of engaging the operator and winning them over. I will add that yes, explanations are important, "Work Smarter - Not Harder" clichés may be helpful, but getting an operator to see *you* as a person can be one of the most useful things you can do.

It should not be necessary to say this, but I will. Acting like that lordly engineer from the "front-office", out among the rabble, explaining to everyone what is best for them, will take you further from your goal than just about anything else you can do. Instead, be personable, friendly, and polite. But above all be professional. And importantly, be interested in what these people have to tell you. (This last, by the way, is not a technique, but in fact the way you learn those, often less than obvious, things which you *really* need to know).

One trick I use to humanize myself is something which stems from a real problem that I have had in the past. When taking a time study, or sometimes just developing an elemental sequence, I have a desire to want to see *everything*. To this end, I would sometimes—without being aware of it—get in too close. I'd find myself hanging over the person's shoulder to see all that their hands are doing, or to evaluate the level of difficulty of an activity, or perhaps to better determine a performance rating.

Believe me, whatever the reason, people *just don't like that!* And so I'm careful not to do it. But also, at some point in the early stages of the analysis or study, if I feel it will be helpful, I warn the associate of my tendency to crowd in, and suggest to them that if I do so, to "just give me a good elbow shot to the ribs" and I'll back off.

This very often gets a laugh, makes me less of a threat, and often opens the door to real cooperation. The goal, again, is go beyond just acceptance, and to create that partnership which I mentioned; So that for a brief while, you *and the subject of your study* co-operate—with the mutual goal of creating a fair work standard. *And incidentally making your own life a bit easier in the process.*

Maintaining Focus

While it is never a bad thing to establish and to maintain an amiable relationship with those whom you are studying, it *is* important to not lose sight of the fact that you have a job to do.

A certain amount of give and take is possible and in fact very useful during the information gathering and documentation process, but don't be distracted while performing a time study. There is a lot to do; clicking the watch at the correct times, entering time observations, noting anomalies, determining a performance rating, and above all watching with a critical eye, and seeing everything—all at pretty much the same time. At this moment, a conversation, or answering questions posed by your subject, or their co-worker(s) is *not* productive.

Members of the workgroup, especially if your relationship with them is amiable, may through thoughtlessness, or intent, act in a way which may disrupt your study. This is not commonplace, but if it does occur, ignore them (politely) or indicate to them (politely) that you are busy. Or, as a last resort, break off the study and explain (politely) why you have stopped and that you're going to begin the exercise all over again.

I am going to mention this once more, for the last time. As you follow the flow of work—collecting information, or taking a study—you must move about to clearly see the work activity as it occurs. Much of the critical activity of an assembly operation is done by the subject's hands. A good clear view of your subject's backside is not usually very helpful. Being in the right place, at the right times, will of course allow for better observations. At the same time, it is *vitally* important that you not get in the way. Not only does this corrupt elemental times if you are taking a study, but very little that you do will irritate an assembler—focused on the work, and performing at an incentive pace—more than the need to pause, and wait for the time study guy to get the **** out of the way, mumbling apologies as they do so.

In light of this, it is usually quite helpful—if you haven't already done so—to watch a cycle or two and plan where you're going to be, and when. And as you take your study, keep your head in the game, to again use a sports analogy. Don't lose focus of your primary task, but also retain awareness of the big picture; of where you are, and that—although you are aloof and objective—you are in fact interacting with others.

The "Just One Thing" Question

Before we at last move on to actually discuss balancing an assembly line, I want to briefly mention the subject of process improvements. Like actually measuring work, process improvement is a topic unto itself, and is outside the scope of this book. But it is an activity of which you should be aware in the context of our subject here.

I earlier mentioned my rather simplistic explanation, to curious friends, as to the role of an Industrial Engineer as being a combination of time study man, and efficiency expert. This is true as far as it goes, and the efficiency expert part is concerned with process improvement, including the introduction of better tooling, and enhanced layout, and more efficient work methods, which of course lead to reduced elemental times (remember the old saw "work smarter, not harder). And so I want to take a moment here to add one more simple technique to your bag of tricks.

Process improvement is not a part of documentation. But for reasons which should be obvious, improvements need to occur in the beginning stages of a project. Process improvement is certainly not a part of work measurement, but changes, if they are to occur at all, must be made before timing begins. Additionally, changes which improve the work environment, or the work performed may also enhance your relationship with the subjects of your studies. And finally, process improvement is not a part of line balancing. Or is it? It can be argued that a better balance is, in fact, a very definite improvement in the overall process.

So I want to close out this section, dealing with the relationship between the IE and those are who studied and measured, by offering this suggestion. In the course of the initial documentation, after you have established at least a grudging working relationship with a member of the workgroup, ask of them this simple question, "Tell me just one thing, just one, which will make things better for you".

Everyone, at every workstation, will have *something* that they wish they had, or that they wish could be made better about their working environment, or the work that they are doing. Some answers you receive can be so pie-in-the-sky as to be rejected out of hand. And usually those offering these suggestions will know it. So a simple explanation as to why that's just not practical is usually accepted.

But many suggestions are good ones, but are often thought by supervisors and engineers (those not actually doing the work) to be frivolous or insignificant, and lip service is paid to the solution but no action is ever taken. Surprisingly often, however, those requests may be accomplished without too much effort on your part.

Some years ago, the company at which I was working produced agricultural equipment. The project which brought me to this company was a reorganization and balance of the line building transmission boxes for large tractors. Several of the line stations were in fact small presses where the various transmission shafts were constructed and queued for use on the line.

Along with pressing gears and bearings onto the shafts, sealing rings were assembled to various shaft grooves. One of the assemblers told me that this latter task would be better accomplished if he had a small, pointed tool, like an Awl, but despite repeated requests it could not get such a tool supplied.

Later that afternoon, I went to a local hardware store and purchased several such tools. The next morning I handed them out to the press stations, and suddenly— despite being the time study guy—I was a hero. My reputation became one of someone who could get things done, and cared enough about the guys on the line to do them. As a result of this one act the remainder of my time in that assembly department was not only less challenging, but I believe more productive.

So ask the question. If it's something you can accomplish, make it your mission to do so. If the request is a good one, but needs management involvement, carry it forward and see if you can't make it happen. If not, don't just forget about it, return to the line and explain why it's just not feasible at this time. Again the perception is that you cared, and at least you tried.

Part Three

The Technique of Line Balance

1. Preparation

Introduction

As has been previously mentioned, an assembly line may be as simple as a balanced, multi-station process combining two or more work stations in a sequential process to build a unit. The extreme opposite of this is a long, extremely complex entity such as an automotive assembly line. A serpentine layout with "feeder" sub-assembly lines—such as a multi-station dashboard line providing (or feeding) completed sub-assemblies to just the right place in the primary process.

Like the actual mechanics of work measurement, the creation and physical set-up of an assembly line are outside the scope of this book. The layout, conveyors, benches, tooling, machinery, if any, test equipment, and such features are by tradition the tasks of manufacturing or facilities engineers, though the input of industrial engineering is—or should be—considered to be of some value. And so you may find yourself a part of the development and set-up activities.

One thing to note is that thinking of, or referring to an assembly line as an actual straight line can often be misleading. "Line" in this context is derived from the term "linear process," in the sense that one work station follows another "down the line." But a station may follow the previous in any direction, literally from anywhere to anywhere. Lines can, and often do turn corners. A line may be U-shaped and finish, more or less, where it began. Lines sometimes divide themselves into two identical work stations to accommodate fixed processes, such as a test cycle, which is greater than the Takt time, only to converge again at the next station.

Lines can be "feeder lines" producing completed sub-assemblies, which are then added to the unit on the larger main line. In another auto-plant example, major sub-assembly lines (frame line and body line)—each complex in their own right—merge to form the final line. There are many more examples. In these postmodern times, "outside the box" thinking is encouraged, and line configuration need be limited only by the nature of the product and by human imagination.

Notwithstanding all of the above, we are going to keep it simple. This book focuses on the understanding and techniques of balancing work between stations in a single contiguous process; whether a complete assembly line, a feeder line, or a designated "zone" within a larger line[3]. In other words, we are going to stick with the basics. These fundamental principles may later be applied, as necessary, to the most complex situations.

If you become involved in the set-up of the physical line itself, you will find this can be interesting and challenging work. However, regardless of your involvement, the project will eventually reach the point at which we begin this discussion. The

---

[3] *No matter how complex, lines may be subdivided into what are often referred to as "zones," each zone being balanced individually to a common Takt time, and each looking remarkably like the simple, straightforward process we will be discussing here.*

time comes to calculate the number of work stations needed to meet the stated demand and to distribute the elements of work more or less equally among them. This means transforming the work content of the linear process, which we have documented and measured, into a multi-station assembly line process—and then to balance it.

The Terminology

Before we discuss the actual balancing, however, let's take a moment to understand the terminology. I refer to those words that are so cavalierly tossed about, especially by the "lean" experts—the non-industrial engineers (IE's) who have tried to usurp some traditional IE functions, applying new age classroom solutions to methodologies that have been successfully used and improved by IE's for more than 100 years, and which are still applicable today.

Like most endeavors, assembly balancing has its own jargon, words with meanings specific to this activity, or which represent concepts that must be grasped for the activity to be successful. An imperfect understanding of the underlying principles may lead to a less than optimal line-balance solution.

Discussion of this terminology brings us to the first phase of the line-balance exercise, a final gathering of all the information needed to organize the line and proceed. In the following pages, we will not only define the terms but also explore the genesis of the numbers that those terms represent. At this point, some are known to us, some are not and must be calculated from those we do know.

Of the following terms, four are what I consider to be "key numbers," which are necessary in the basic organization of the line. A brief glossary of necessary terms follows. Each will be expanded upon in the following sections.

— Total Work Content (TWC)—Key Number

TWC is simply the total amount of time required to produce one complete unit. In other words, it is the sum of all elemental times, as documented in the sequence of events. TWC is the first of the key numbers. It is a necessary factor in determining the required number of work stations.

– Demand (D)—Key Number

Sometimes called "customer demand," this is the number of complete units that the line is required to produce in a given amount of time. (See Available Minutes per Shift.) Demand is usually determined by Marketing, and passed down via Production Management or Scheduling, or, in the case of a feeder line, the number of units required by its "customer," the main line. For reasons I think to be obvious, the number of units required is also a key number.

– Takt (or Takt Time) (T)—Key Number

Takt is the amount of time within which *each* unit must be completed in order to meet a stated demand—within a specified number of available minutes. For example, if the available time is 480 minutes and the stated demand is

48 units, the Takt time is 10 minutes. (This key number is the primary building block by which the line is organized, and is the product of a calculation.)

– Total Mins/Shift (TM/S)

TM/S is the total number of minutes per one work shift. This is often 480 minutes (for example 7:00 am to 3:30 pm, if a lunch break is not counted). This number may be literally any amount of time, based on local practices, or if overtime is considered. TM/S is required to calculate available minutes per shift.

– Available Mins/Shift (AM/S)—Key Number

AM/S is the actual number of minutes in one shift that are available for production. AM/S is determined by subtracting all work stoppages (downtime) from the total minutes per shift. (This last of the key numbers is also the product of a calculation.)

– Downtime (D/T)

Anticipated Downtime, or Planned Downtime, is the result of scheduled line stoppages such as morning and afternoon breaks, end of shift clean-up, department meetings, and other such non-productive times, which regularly occur during the shift.

Unanticipated Downtime, or Unplanned Downtime. It must be recognized that, despite the best efforts of all involved, a certain amount of time *will* be lost in any given work period, owing to unplanned stoppages such as minor machinery breakdown, unit repair, material shortages, and a host of other problems, many of which may be insignificant in isolation but can, and sometimes do add up to a significant amount of time.

Not only is this fact the bane of supervisors and production management, but also the random nature of such unplanned stoppages makes calculating this number with any degree of certainty very difficult. Moving lines may track stoppages, if the monitors exist. But, more often, historical data—and occasionally an educated guess—will result in an agreed-upon percentage by which available minutes are, for planning purposes, reduced.

Author's note: Everyone involved—management, supervision, and line associates—benefits from the reduction of unplanned downtime, and should be "on the lookout" for ways to eliminate what the "lean" folks rightly call waste.

– Average Minutes/Work Station (WSA)

Average minutes/station (WSA) is total work content (TWC) divided by the calculated (or pre-determined) number of work stations. This very significant value is the number to which the line is actually balanced. (WSA is a calculated number.)

– Cycle Time

Often mistakenly confused with Takt time or WSA, the cycle time of any given work station is the amount of elemental time that is (after balancing) assigned to that work station. As a result of work assignments, one station will always have the longest cycle time. Thanks to Eli Goldratt's excellent and groundbreaking book, *The Goal*, this station is now almost universally referred to as "the bottleneck."

When the line is adequately balanced, with average minutes/station below the Takt time, station cycle time is a fairly insignificant number. If the line itself is said to have a cycle time, it is equal to the amount of time assigned to the bottleneck station, as no completed unit may exit the line faster than it can pass through the slowest work station.

Author's note: The Goal, *by Eli Goldratt, introduced to the world the management philosophy known as the Theory of Constraints. If you are interested in or involved with synchronous production systems, and if you have not read the book already, I strongly recommend you do so. Entertainingly written as a novel,* The Goal *introduces you to Alex, Jonah, and, importantly, Herbie.*

– Utilization

Expressed as a percentage, utilization is a measure of the total amount of work assigned to the line vs. the time available (or capacity) to the line in which to do that work.

Additional Terminology

The above terms are pretty much standard everywhere. To this list, I would like to add a few terms of my own, which come into play as we begin to actually create a balance.

– Work Content Additions

After determining the number of work stations needed to meet demand, it may be necessary to add additional work elements to the sequence of events. Depending upon circumstance, extra elements (for example, moving the unit to the next station) may be necessary at some or all work stations, the exact number of which is unknown until calculated, as described above. If required, these and other "station specific" work elements need to be added where applicable.

– Elemental Restrictions

Some things must happen when they do, and as such are unalterable milestones in the process. These elements, once positioned, either in initial line set-up or in first elemental allocations, may be mostly ignored in further balance activities. Their importance lies now in how other work may be or may need to be organized around them.

– Elemental Dependencies

Earlier, I commented on how the making of the balance "levels" station times by moving bits of work (and thus time) between stations, while maintaining the linear integrity of the process. It is here that the concept comes into play.

A significant number of work elements must of necessity occur either after or before some major event. (For example, an engine cover may not be mounted before placement of the engine, but must occur *before* a structural member positioned above the cover may be installed.)

– Balancers

Within the ranks of the dependent elements are what I refer to as "balancers." These are work elements representing comparatively small amounts of time, which may be performed virtually anywhere within a range of work stations.

Like all work elements, these tasks must of course occur before some actions and after others. For balancer elements, the range is generally wider, and with more freedom of placement. As such, these bits of time are what I look for and utilize to "fine-tune" a balance.

2. The Calculations

Introduction

In this section, we will discuss the calculations needed to utilize the information we know, to calculate the remaining key numbers we need to organize and balance the line. For the purposes of the following examples, we will assume these numbers:

Total work content (TWC) 62.84 mins Available mins/shift (AM/S) Unknown at this time

Demand (D) 50 units

No. of work stations Unknown

Total mins/shift (TM/S) 480 mins

Takt Unknown at this time

Anticipated downtime (D/T) 25 mins

Unanticipated D/T 6.25 %

The Key Numbers

Demand (D) is known to us as the required number of units that must be produced within the available time. Demand is usually determined by Marketing or Management.

TWC is the sum of all elemental Minutes in the Sequence of Events.

AM/S is, at the start of our calculations, not known, and must be calculated from several known data, including TM/S, minus the sum of all anticipated (scheduled) and unanticipated line stoppages. AM/S is calculated as in the following example:

TM/S	*480 mins*	
Minus:		
Anticipated D/T		
Start of shift meeting	*5 mins*	
AM break	*10 mins*	
Pre-lunch clean-up	*5 mins*	
PM break	*10 mins*	
End of shift clean-up	<u>*5 mins*</u>	
	25 mins	
		= 455 mins
Minus:		
Unanticipated D/T (6.25%)		
455 mins x .0625 = 28.44 mins		

AM/S	*= 426.56 mins*

Takt time, often simply **Takt**, is possibly the most misunderstood—and certainly the most misused—term of them all. I've often heard and read of Takt time being described as the "cycle time" of a work station or of the line. Alternatively, it is sometimes said to be the time allowed for each work station to complete its work (closer, but still not true).

Takt is derived from the German word *Taktzeit*, which is translated in various ways, all of which mean pretty much the same thing. One (my favorite) is "rhythm." Others such as "tempo" and "pace," and even the metaphorical notion of an orchestra conductor's baton, moving to and fro to mark time, have been used to explain the meaning of the word Takt, and how it applies to an assembly line. All, to some degree, are appropriate.

The actual meaning of the word Takt, as applied to an assembly line, is the amount of time in which each unit must be completed in order to meet a stated demand within a given period of time. Takt time is one of several of what I refer to as "key numbers"—those bits of information that are fundamental to the basic organization of the work content on the assembly line. Takt time does—in a way—define the line's rhythm, as all work stations must be assigned an amount of work (again, measured in time), which is very near to, but does not exceed Takt.

Takt time is the result of a calculation, one component of which, demand (D), is known or supplied. One, available minutes/shift (AM/S), is not, and must itself be calculated before Takt can be determined. The Takt time calculation is this:

$$\frac{Available\ minutes/shift\ (AM/S)}{Demand\ (D)}$$

We know that D = 50 units, and, having calculated AM/S, we now have the information needed to calculate Takt time (T). Thus,

$$T = \frac{426.56\ mins\ (AM/S)}{50\ units\ (D)} = 8.53\ mins$$

Number of Work Stations

Now that we have determined Takt time to be 8.53 mins, we can go on to calculate the number of assembly line work stations required to produce 50 units in the available time of 426.56 mins.

Author's note: Takt time is important. In fact, it is vital. As has been noted, it is a key number, fundamental for the determination of the required number of work stations. Also, Takt time serves as a limit on the amount of work that may be assigned to each.

However—contrary to popular opinion—once the number of work stations has been determined, Takt time is no longer a significant factor, as focus now shifts to Average Minutes per Work Station (WSA), *or simply* Average Minutes. *We will explore and explain this reality when we begin to discuss assigning work elements. But first, we need to determine the required number of work stations.*

Once all of the key numbers are known, we can begin to transform the sequence of events—which we have spent so much time developing and refining—into a synchronous, multi-station production process, in other words, an assembly line. The next calculation, that of determining the number of work stations needed, is the simple, straightforward, and, I should think, fairly obvious, exercise shown below.

$$\frac{Total\ work\ content\ (TWC)}{Takt\ (T)} = No.\ of\ work\ stations$$

We know TWC, how much time it takes to build one complete unit, to be 62.40 mins. As the result of the previous calculations, we now know Takt time to be 8.53 mins. So we can determine the required number of work stations thus:

$$\frac{62.40\ mins\ (TWC)}{8.53\ mins\ (T)} = 7.37 = 8\ work\ stations$$

For reasons which again should be obvious, we cannot organize the assembly line with a partial work station. So the calculated number must always be rounded *up* to the next whole work station. In this example, we would organize this process with eight work stations. Recalling our earlier discussion, this number represents not eight physical locations on the line, but rather eight persons to whom work may be assigned.

Average Minutes per Station (WSA)

Deceptively simple to calculate, average minutes per station (WSA) is nonetheless a very important number as we reach the point of actually assigning work. The calculation for this value is shown below:

$$\frac{62.40\ mins\ (TWC)}{8\ work\ stations} = 7.80\ average\ mins/work\ station$$

The Balance Chart below, showing a hypothetical balance, demonstrates the relationship between Takt time and average minutes per station.

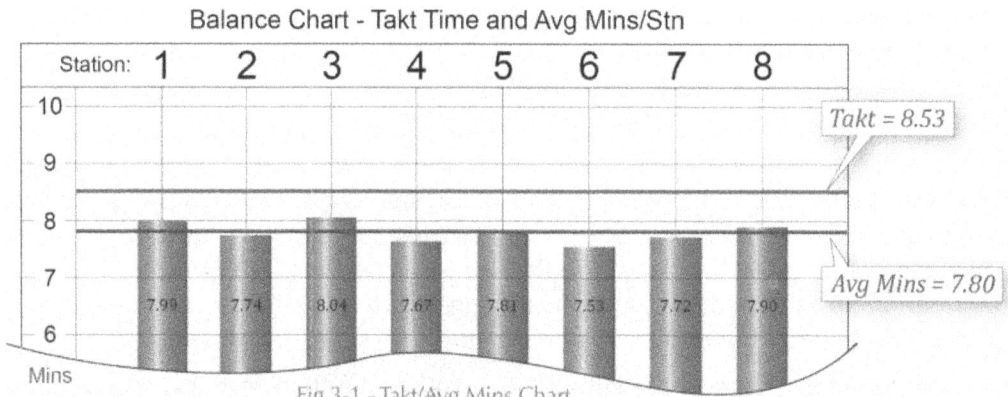

Fig 3-1 - Takt/Avg Mins Chart

3. Line Organization

Introduction

With the calculations completed, all the required organizational information is now known. Takt time—the most significant key number in getting to this point—now becomes less important. The goal of the balance exercise is to distribute all work elements (and their associated times) more or less evenly over what we now know to be the required number of stations. THE number to which those times are distributed—or balanced—is the average minutes per station, or simply average minutes (WSA).

In the balancing process, work elements are assigned and reassigned until the work load (time) deviation of each station to WSA is as small as possible. If we have calculated the correct number of work stations, and WSA for all stations falls within an acceptable range—some station times lower than average and some above—*all* work station times will be less than the Takt time. This, in simple terms, is "the balance."

The rule to follow is: "Organize to Takt time—balance to average time."

The station to which the *most* time is assigned is referred to as the "high station" or the "bottleneck." It is of utmost importance that the high station time of the completed balance does not exceed Takt time. We will discuss some methodologies for getting to that completed balance in the following sections.

But first, after determining the number of work stations and calculating the average time that may be assigned to each, we must pause and take a moment to examine the new line with an eye both to utilization and to potential problems that may arise from the station-to-station time deviation.

Utilization and the Bottleneck

Earlier, it was stated that a line's utilization is a measure of work assigned vs. the time available in which to do that work. The example in the previous section shows the relationship between average mins/station and Takt. In that hypothetical example, average mins = 7.80 mins, while Takt = 8.53 mins. A simple calculation tells us that the utilization = 91.4%.

The desire for a high utilization percentage notwithstanding, the difference between Takt and average minutes must be sufficient to allow for the variations—inherent in virtually any balance—in the amount of work assigned to each station, and still ensure that the high station (or bottleneck) remains below Takt. In industrial engineering parlance, the smaller the deviation between work stations, the "tighter" the balance. The tightest balance—the smallest station-to-station deviation from average minutes—is, of course, the most desirable solution.

However, there are practical limits to our ability to achieve a perfect or near-perfect balance. For this reason, an overall +/- of 5% is generally considered to be acceptable. Therefore, average minutes should, as a guideline, be at least 5% lower than Takt.

The key numbers—Takt, number of work stations, and average minutes per station —are determined by the calculations, using the situational data as it exists. These are hard numbers, the result of manufacturing circumstances beyond your control, and may not be arbitrarily altered to achieve a desired utilization percentage. An axiom that is always good to remember is, "A thing is what it is, not what you want it to be."

And it is certainly possible that these calculations may result in an unacceptably high utilization, making it impossible to limit high station time to the Takt time. It is also possible that the utilization percentage is OK, but that subsequent necessary additions to the sequence of events (and therefore TWC) may raise the utilization to an unacceptable level.

Adding Work Content

We develop an initial sequence of events as if one person were building the product, from start to finish. Transforming this sequence of events into an assembly line process adds an important factor—additional line personnel needed to accomplish the required work in the required time to meet demand. And with them come additional work content.

Elements such as "Move unit into first station" must always take place before work can begin, and may thus be included at the beginning of the documented process in the initial sequence of events. On the other hand, "Move unit to the next station" may or may not occur after work is completed in each additional work station. These and other such "station specific" required tasks must be added to the work content of the line, and this can be done only after the total number of work stations has been determined. They cannot be planned for in the initial sequence of events for the simple reason that we don't at that time know how many work stations we're going to end up with. So, once we do know, it's time to insert them in the process—and this of course increases total work content.

If we are fortunate, the addition won't alter the line organization that we have just determined. It is somewhat unlikely that the number of work stations will have to be altered. But it is certainly possible—especially with a longer line (the more stations, the more additional work)—that the added work content will raise average minutes unacceptably close to the Takt time. So, it becomes necessary at this point to recalculate and to know for certain just where our line organization stands.

If the WSA becomes, as a result of additions, sufficiently close to, or at or above the Takt time, it will be virtually impossible to balance the overall line without the high station time (and perhaps that of others as well) becoming greater than Takt.

As it is impossible for completed units to exit the line at a pace faster than the bottleneck station, the required demand cannot be achieved. If presented with such a circumstance, what are we to do?

Adding a Work Station

The simplest remedy (on paper, at least) is to add one work station to the line and balance to the new average minutes. In practical terms, however, this may prove to be the most difficult option. Aside from the potential difficulties involved in physically accommodating an additional person and potential work area and material presentation issues, that person will significantly increase the labor cost of a unit.

Additionally, an extra station resulting from a relatively small increase in TWC will result in an unfavorably low WSA when compared to Takt time. Per-person and line utilization will suffer dramatically as a result, making even a good balance a nonetheless very inefficient one. Believe me, in this circumstance, resistance to adding a person to the line will be substantial, and it is likely to come from several directions at once.

Alternate Solutions

If we cannot, or should not, add a station, what are the alternatives? Let's go back to the reason the situation exists in the first place, which arises from the relative key numbers—total work content, demand, and available minutes. If one or more of these numbers are not changed, the result, that is to say, not meeting demand, is a foregone conclusion, and all of the encouragement, cajoling, wishing and hoping, at any level, will not help (I say this because the number(s) *must* be changed in some way, and only the management can make that happen).

Changing any one of the key numbers is a management decision and action. Do we reduce demand? Probably unlikely, unless you're building products to be put into a warehouse. But the question is worth asking. Perhaps the number Marketing came up with is an estimate. Maybe a little additional research on their part might provide the solution. In any case, it is certainly not the engineer's decision to make.

Reduce total work content? Cost reduction projects are ongoing, or should be, but it's probably unwise to set up the line just in the hope that you can meet the schedule by instantly finding a way to reduce production time sufficiently. As an industrial engineer, I would encourage you to keep those projects moving. Sooner or later, they will pay off.

That leaves the most flexible of the key numbers—available minutes. Work rules, number and duration of breaks and clean-up times, and so forth are probably contractual and not easily changed, even if it might be a good idea to do so. However, the duration of the shift is flexible. And you're in this situation because your numbers are probably very close to, or at the cusp. So, it is possible that just a few extra hours, once in a while, carefully monitored, will keep you right on schedule.

Low Utilization

As likely as it is to be confronted with an unacceptably high utilization percentage, it is also possible for the calculated average minutes to be too low. If WSA is very low, as compared to Takt, the line is inherently inefficient, and utilization is poor. The result is a considerable amount of lost time (waste) at every work station.

Production could be increased, of course, but demand has been established, and, in a time when building to inventory is often considered to be a negative, this may be an unacceptable option. Reducing available minutes is an option, although it would mean both personal and physical resources possibly being idled. And altering TWC to *add* work (and thus, cost) seems a bit counterproductive.

Finally, it *may* be possible to actually reduce the number of work stations by one. However, if key number calculations are correct, this would lead to an unacceptably *high* utilization percentage, putting us back to where we were in the previous discussion. But if the new utilization number is not excessively high and there is the ability to apply alternate solutions as mentioned above, the economic benefits of removing a whole work station could (and I stress the word *could*) quite possibly outweigh the negatives. This action must be considered carefully for all of its ramifications, and would need to be approved at a higher management level.

Author's note: The foregoing discussion is not meant to offer definitive solutions, but merely to suggest possibilities. I have no doubt that there are other acceptable and viable remedies, of which I am not aware, for the situations described. My purpose here is to convey the belief that there almost certainly are solutions, and that the engineer often needs to be creative and keep an open mind.

Throughput and Simultaneous Operations

Throughput (or throughput time) can be a vitally important measure to some, not so much to others. It is dependent on local business imperatives, which usually determine the goals of the production line within a given organization.

Throughput (TP) is, simply, the actual amount of time it takes any single unit to travel from its first assembly element to the moment it leaves the line as a completed assembly.

Important to this discussion, total work content (TWC) is the amount of time required to produce one complete unit, as assembled in a single station or in a series of work stations (i.e., an assembly line).

The opportunities for reducing throughput time depend, of course, on the nature of the product itself. Some products offer many possibilities. Some products do not. Below is a simplified scenario of a line producing generator units, demonstrating a dramatic reduction in throughput. Please note that, while the work stations have been moved and the timeline reduced, the linear sequence remains unchanged.

In a contiguous assembly line, TWC and TP time are equal. However, TP may be possibly be reduced. This is potentially important because, while TWC and, by extension, labor cost remain the same, reducing the actual time needed to produce a finished product—with the same amount of resources—has several benefits.

Utilization of the line and its facilities is increased. More units may be produced in a given elapsed time. If the line is building to customer demand, units may be produced and, importantly, delivered in a shorter time, a powerful advantage in sales.

Throughput - Straight Line vs Optimized Line

Frame	Wire Harness	Prep Engine-1	Prep Engine-2	Mount Engine	Prep Fuel Tank	Mount Fuel Tank	Final Assy
1 1.50 m	**2** 1.35 m	**3** 1.40 m	**4** 1.35 m	**5** 1.55 m	**6** 1.45 m	**7** 1.50 m	**8** 1.45 m

$TWC = 11.55$

$Avg\ Mins = 1.44$

(Elapsed Time per Unit) Thruput = 11.55

Prep Fuel Tank
6 1.45 m

Frame	Wire Harness		Mount Fuel Tank	Final Assy
1 1.50 m	**2** 1.35 m	**5** 1.55 m	**7** 1.50 m	**8** 1.45 m

3 1.40 m — **4** 1.35 m → Mount Engine

Prep Engine-1 | Prep Engine-2
1.50 m | 1.35 m | 1.55 m | 1.50 m | 1.45 m

$TWC = 11.55$

$Avg\ Mins = 1.49$

(Elapsed Time per Unit) Thruput = 7.45

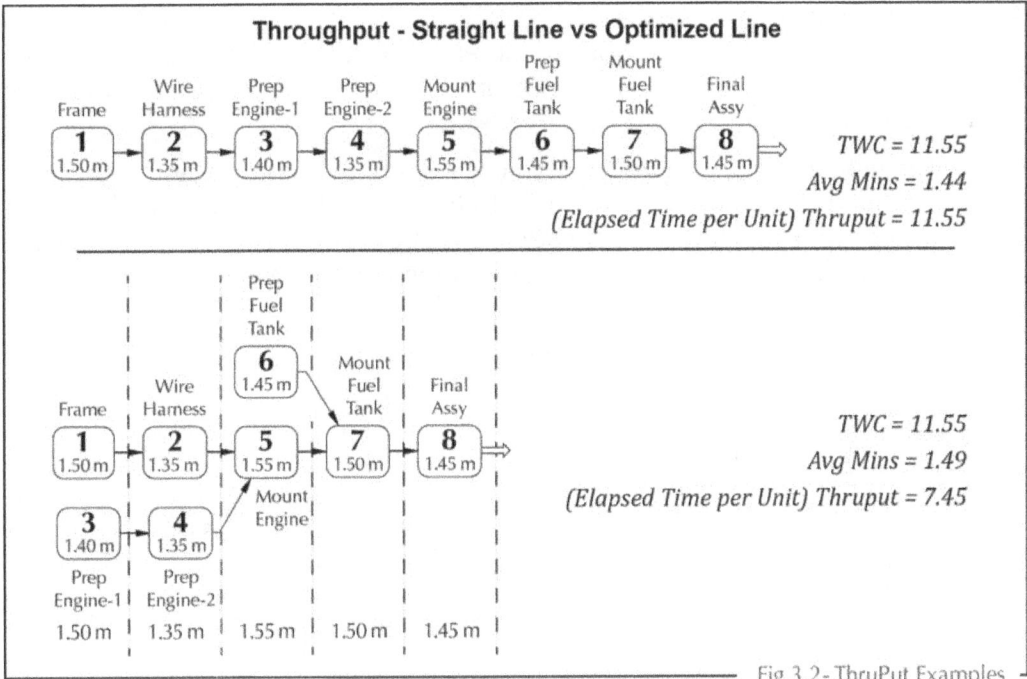

Fig 3.2 - ThruPut Examples

As mentioned above, for any number of reasons (the nature of the product, the physical conditions in which the line exists, business reasons, and so on), throughput reduction may not be possible or necessary. However, the inherent efficiency in simultaneous operations is a core industrial engineering principle, and I would encourage you to keep an open mind to such possibilities.

Final Thoughts: Very Long Lines

It is possible to be assigned to a line (or a portion of a line) that is (dauntingly) long. It can sometimes be helpful to view this line as a series of "zones," as is commonly done in the automobile industry. My experience with auto plants is limited to a somewhat brief project in a plant that produced minivans and SUVs, each within a Takt time of 45 seconds. Needless to say, the pace was intense but impressively well-controlled. The material re-supply was relentless, the staff and, by extension, the number of work stations was very large, and the line itself, from the welding of the bodies to paint, to preliminary assembly, to final assembly, almost unimaginably complex—and long.

So, in that instance, the entire process was subdivided, first by sections: body weld, frame assembly, rough and finish final assembly, as well as a number of feeder lines (i.e., dashboard assembly). Many sections were of such length as to be further divided into "zones," each zone being treated as a line unto itself.

Working with a series of smaller "line" entities makes the balancing of each somewhat more manageable, although, of course, there are more of them. Often sections and perhaps some zones within each section may be assigned to additional engineers, if desired. But remember that all sections and zones are actually part of a *single process*, and each must adhere to the same rules. Takt time and average minutes apply everywhere. A high station that exceeds the Takt time in one zone diminishes the throughput of the entire line, from the placement of the first body component to the movement of the completed unit to the outgoing queue.

While it is unlikely that you will find yourself doing the basic organization of an auto assembly line, it is certainly possible to be assigned to a line of some length; many, if not all such lines contain 20, 30, or more locations with multiple assemblers (work stations). If so, you may find the concept of sections or zones to be helpful.

4. The Balance Process

Introduction

I began thinking about writing this book because there was so very little practical information in the literature on the subject of assembly line balance. But I must emphasize the word *practical*. Actually, the Internet is full of information, provided by the lean culture—and more than a few doctoral candidates—offering increasingly complex methodologies for assigning priorities and precedents to the elements of an assembly process. Accordingly, one or another sophisticated algorithm may then provide the eventual balance solution.

As you may have suspected by now, I'm a bit old-fashioned. I hold the increasingly peculiar notion that the industrial engineer is paid to solve the balance problem, and that the necessary preparation—process documentation and the subsequent measurement of work elements—results in an intimate knowledge of the nature and components of the puzzle. I further believe that, by the time the engineer expends the time and energy to work out and assign said precedents and priorities, he or she may as well just go ahead and do the balance.

Also, consider that the priorities of process landmarks and most major elements are, for the most part, already determined in the process development stage, when the assembly sequence is first determined and stabilized. These major process steps may of course be altered, revised, supplemented, or even eliminated as the product (and process) matures as a result of design change, process improvement, or cost reduction initiatives. However, at the time of the initial balance, the process should be fixed in what is determined to be—at that moment—the "best method." Improvement initiatives lie in the future, often resulting in re-balance activities.

The occasional quantum leap notwithstanding, to imagine and "see" the possibilities of product and process improvement, it is most often necessary to observe and become familiar with the current reality, and then to begin asking that all-important IE question, "I see what is, but WHAT IF... ?".

Author's note: There are two examples I have often used to demonstrate and to back up this belief. First, Henry Ford, the manufacturing process genius of the 20th century, started with the "state-of-the art" Model T. It took much iteration and a long series of better models—and learning a little bit (or sometimes a lot) from each —before the Mustang could make an appearance. Similarly, the Wright brothers did not fly a 747 from the sands of Kitty Hawk. And, although the advance from the Wright Flyer to the jumbo jet took an amazingly short time, there were still many contributors and many, many thousands of small "what if?" steps in between.

So, we create and optimize a balance from the best process available at the moment, confident that an ongoing series of improvements will evolve from today's best efforts.

In my view, assembly line balancing, like many other aspects of IE work, is something of a "soft science," requiring perhaps less formal education and a certain amount of on-the-job experience. Like time study and other forms of work measurement, the skills and the "art" are often still passed down from the old-timers to the neophytes, such as I once was.

After the revolution in IE, lean experts felt the need to take over administration of the manufacturing process. And, being mostly intellectuals and academics, many of these new "experts" turned to technology and a formalized methodology full of (mostly Japanese) buzzwords and key phrases by which the heart of many traditional IE practices were to be mechanized.

Author's note: To be fair, a number of useful methodologies and insightful ways of viewing the process were unquestionably introduced in this period as well. My position, however, is that these new techniques enhanced the role of the IE, rather than replaced it.

Moving, at last, to the balancing process itself, we find the initial stages of the exercise to be straightforward and simple. It is the final stage of the balance—that last, subtle fine-tuning, the real heart of the puzzle—that most requires a thorough knowledge of product and process, imagination, and the desire (and the ability) to solve the puzzle—exactly what we, as IE's, like to do.

Getting Started

As has been previously noted, and by now belabored, the starting point of the balance preparation can be documenting an established line that needs merely a re-balance to a different number of work stations. Or it may be a new process, still in development, lacking refined methods, times, and even—from the manufacturing engineer's point of view—proper tooling.

In either circumstance, or any in between, the starting point of the balance exercise is a completed sequence of events; the single, linear series of work elements required to build the product—as it will be done from here on.

The assembly process has, at this point, been established and documented in a logical, do-able sequence. The development of the physical line, however, often begins with a mostly empty space—or, as I usually refer to it, "some tables and a pile of parts." The detailed line layout must actually wait at least until the fundamental balance information, including the number of work stations, has been calculated (or sometimes pre-determined). However, to organize work stations and set them up with the required equipment and tools and stock them with the correct materials in the correct places, we must first determine what work is to be done where.

The space itself has been allocated and prepared, and the major "landmark" equipment is in place—or at least the locations are designated. But the essence of the balance is the arrangement of smaller work elements, achieving the most effective, efficient, and of course most productive sequence. Thus, the final line set up must usually wait until a balance has been established

The initial balancing task, then—after determining the correct *number* of stations—is to divide the sequence of work elements into a number of discrete lists, each representing the work content of a single station. The next task is to level, or balance, the work so that each station contains a total time that is as close as possible to average minutes per station; all while (importantly) maintaining the linear integrity of the process. We have finally reached the point of setting up, and hence beginning to solve the puzzle.

A few final thoughts before we begin. The final balance often represents the ultimate in the game of "what if?". Viewed as a chart, the unbalanced line will present either "high points," from which time must be removed, or what I call "holes," which must be filled with, of course, time.

It is important to keep in mind that revisions to station times must necessarily be taken in pairs. Any movement of an element of work will impact two stations—where the work comes from and where it moves to. These stations need not be contiguous. But also remember, we may now be altering the linear process, so I think I'm safe in saying that rule number one when moving elements, forward or back, over other elements is that the process must remain viable.

A somewhat extreme example would be to establish a perfect time in two stations, by moving the element "mount and secure fuel tank" to a place in the process after the element "fill fuel tank." There will probably be many such possibilities for ill-advised elemental movements (some much less obvious), and therefore it is always necessary to consider not only time balance but also the practical impact of each considered elemental move.

Step One: Defining the Stations

As with other activities discussed in this book, we will approach the balance puzzle in a series of iterative steps. This approach accomplishes two things. The completion of each step provides a base from which to move forward. Each iteration usually teaches us something about the organizational possibilities that are coming to light, and which will be useful as we proceed.

It has been determined that the line balancing example that follows is to contain four work stations. Step One of the process is to divide our list of process elements (the sequence of events) into a series of four elemental lists, each now representing the work content of its work station.

Revising the overall list of elements into a sequence of individual work station lists is very straightforward, requiring merely a bit of simple arithmetic. Starting with the first work element, move down the sequence of events until the sum of the selected elemental times is (more or less) at the previously calculated average minutes. This first list of elements is then designated as Station 1. Repeat as required.

The elemental sequence, and thus the linear integrity of the process, has not changed. We have merely added station breaks. Having done so, we can now add the station specific elements discussed earlier. The revised elemental list will now look something like this.

Medium Platform w/Extension	KL-1003482-002		Stn:	1
Station 1: Mount Frame to Line		Line: B17	Mins/Stn:	3.147
	Element Description			Mins.
1	Load Frame from Queue to Line Work Station 1 w/Hoist			1.321
2	Attach Nameplate to Frame w/(4) Pop Rivits			0.381
3	Attach Logo Plate to Frame w/(2) Pop Rivits		2.936	0.223
4	Assemble Frame Cross-Member to Frame w/(16) Screws			1.011
5	Advance Unit to Station 2 Fig 3-3-1		+ .211	0.211

Medium Platform w/Extension	KL-1003482-002		Stn:	2
Station 2: Tighten Frame X-Member		Line: B17	Mins/Stn:	2.240
	Element Description			Mins.
6	Tighten (16) Cross-Member Screws w/Power Tool			0.521
7	Torque (16) Cross-Member Screws and Mark			0.589
8	Assemble Valve Mounting Plate to Frame w/(4) Screws - w/Power Tool			0..466
9	Torque (4) Mounting Plate Screws and Mark		2.029	0.329
10	Mount Cylinder Valve to Mtg Plate w/(3) Screws			0.401
11	Torque (2) Cylinder Valve Screws and Mark			0.189
12	Advance Unit to Station 3 Fig 3-3-2		+ .211	0.211

Medium Platform w/Extension	KL-1003482-002		Stn:	3
Station 3: Hydraulic Tubes		Line: B17	Mins/Stn:	2.135
	Element Description			Mins.
13	Loose Assemble (2) Hydr Tube Clamps to Frame R/S Wall			0.363
14	Position (2) Hydr Tubes into R/S Wall Clamps			0.281
15	Align (2) Tubes and tighten (2) Clamps w/Power Tool		1.924	0.366
16	Asbl Supply Hose from Valve (Port A) to Upper Hydr Tube (Aft End) and Tighten			0.457
17	Asbl Return Hose from Valve (Port B) to Lower Hydr Tube (Aft End) and Tighten			0.457
18	Advance Unit to Station 4 Fig 3-3-3		+ .211	0.211

Medium Platform w/Extension	KL-1003482-002		Stn:	4
Station 4: Final Assy		Line: B17	Mins/Stn:	2.144
	Element Description			Mins.
19	Assemble R/S Extension Support to top of Frame w/(2) Screws			0.378
20	Assemble L/S Extension Support to top of Frame w/(2) Screws			0.378
21	Torque (4) Extension Support Screws and Mark		1.842	0.519
22	Torque (2) Hydr Hose Connectors (Both Ends) and Mark			0.389
23	Mark Sub-Assembly Sequence Number to Frame			0.178
24	Move Completed Sub-Assembly to Main Line Fig 3-3-4		+ .302	0.302

Determining station break points also provides a good demonstration of the benefits of the "smallest transferable element" rule. But still, elemental times will vary, sometimes dramatically, and the individual station times will vary as well.

Further using the spreadsheet, we have the ability to "see" the balance puzzle both as tabular data and/or in graphic format, as shown for the initial (rough) balance in Fig. 3-4.

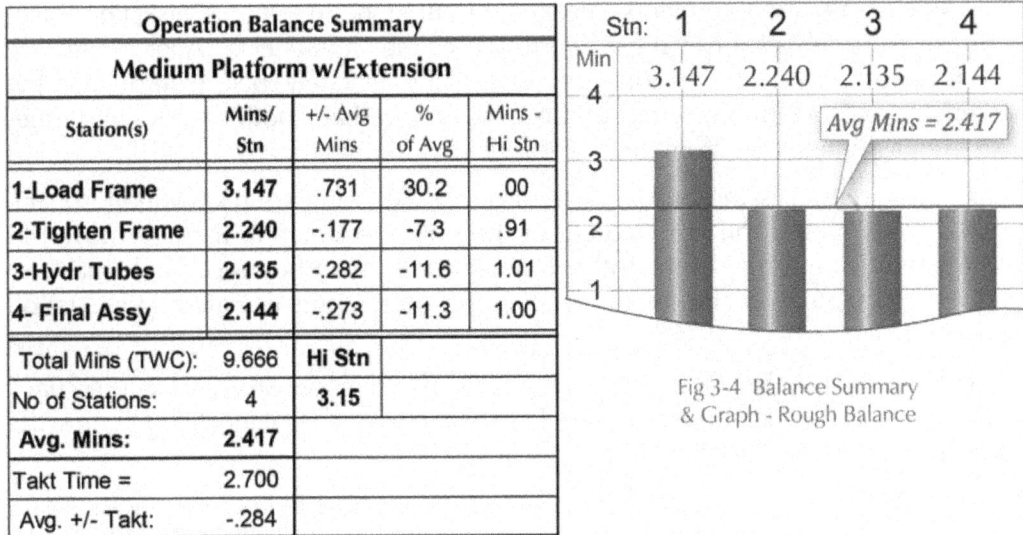

Operation Balance Summary						Stn: 1 2 3 4
Medium Platform w/Extension					
Station(s)	Mins/ Stn	+/- Avg Mins	% of Avg	Mins - Hi Stn	
1-Load Frame	3.147	.731	30.2	.00	
2-Tighten Frame	2.240	-.177	-7.3	.91	
3-Hydr Tubes	2.135	-.282	-11.6	1.01	
4- Final Assy	2.144	-.273	-11.3	1.00	
Total Mins (TWC):	9.666	Hi Stn			
No of Stations:	4	3.15			
Avg. Mins:	2.417				
Takt Time =	2.700				
Avg. +/- Takt:	-.284				

Min 4 3.147 2.240 2.135 2.144
Avg Mins = 2.417
3
2
1

Fig 3-4 Balance Summary & Graph - Rough Balance

As the balance exercise proceeds through some or perhaps many iterations, the tabular and graphic information will provide real-time results for each elemental move. This instant feedback is invaluable for maintaining momentum in solving the puzzle.

Author's note: In the "old days", when each work element and its time value were recorded on an index card (or even a strip of paper), the game of playing "what if?" with the reassignment of elements—which is the heart of the balance exercise— meant physically rearranging the cards with each move.

I found that I can hold only three or four moves (and the associated arithmetic) in my head before starting to lose track. So I was now forced to recalculate, resorting to the tedious process of using an adding machine. I could then either accept this "new" balance or go forward from there—or even put it all back the way it was and start over.

It is this activity that I long ago dubbed the "grunt work" of assembly line balance. In this bright new age, we still follow the old methodology of moving elements about, but using a spreadsheet makes the task not only easier but much quicker.

Adding a "Header" to each work station list completes Step One, establishing the rough balance. We can now use this information as the starting point for Step Two.

Step Two: Leveling the Stations

Step Two of the balance process is what I think of as the "leveling phase." This step is also quite simple. Using the chart and/or the tabular balance data, identify the work stations with the highest and correspondingly lowest times. Then, make initial adjustments by what is, in effect, simply moving station break points.

We begin by identifying the high station. To do this, simply find the work station to which the largest amount of work (measured in time, not number of tasks) has been assigned. This high station is often referred to as the "bottleneck." After identifying the bottleneck, look at the adjacent stations immediately before and after the bottleneck, and determine which of these two (or perhaps both) will benefit time-wise from assuming time from the bottleneck.

If the lower station is the one after the bottleneck, using your knowledge of the process, determine if the last element of the bottleneck station may be moved to become the first element of the following station. If it can be moved, relocate it to be the first element in the next station, and note the recalculated work station times.[4]

If it is determined to be necessary or otherwise effective to instead move time back to the previous work station, move the first element of the bottleneck to become the last element of the previous station.

It may, of course, be necessary—if possible—to move time in both directions. There is no limit to how many elements, from either the beginning or the end of the work station, can be moved to achieve the goal of leveling and bringing each station closer to the average minutes/station. But remember, in Step Two, elements are relocated between stations *without* altering the linear sequence.

A notable thing about bottleneck stations is that, when you reduce work station time and turn a bottleneck into a non-bottleneck, another will instantly take its place. Continue the leveling, or at least consider the possibilities, through the entire list of work stations.

A review of the work station times reveals that Station 1 contains the most time and is the bottleneck. Total work content and number of stations have determined that the AM/S = 2.417 minutes. This time +/- 5% per station is our goal throughout the balancing process. And we immediately notice that the Station 1 time created in Step One far exceeds this goal.

Needing to retain the linear sequence, we are left with but one option. After consulting with the manufacturing engineer and the line supervisor, we agree that there is no mechanical or logistical reason why the frame cross-member cannot be added to the frame in the following station. So Element 4 is moved to become Element 1 of Station 2. This reduces the Station 1 time to 1.136 minutes. This is a bit low, but OK for now.

Continuing with our balance example, the actions and the results of the leveling process are shown below in Figs. 3-5-1 to 3-5-4.

---

[4] Note that station specific elements that have been added to the work stations are immune to such moves. After insertion, consider station specific elements to be locked in place.

Medium Platform w/Extension	KL-1003482-002		Stn:	1
Station 1: Mount Frame to Line		Line: B17	Mins/Stn:	2.136
	Element Description			Mins.
1	Load Frame from Queue to Line Work Station 1 w/Hoist			1.321
2	Attach Nameplate to Frame w/(4) Pop Rivits			0.381
3	Attach Logo Plate to Frame w/(2) Pop Rivits			0.223
~~4~~	~~Assemble Frame Cross-Member to Frame w/(16) Screws~~			~~1.011~~
5	Advance Unit to Station 2	Fig 3-5-1		0.211

This move causes Station 2 to immediately assume the role of bottleneck. And its new time is even greater than that of Station 1. (Are we going in the wrong direction? No, wait. We're not yet finished.)

Looking now at Station 2, we see that the last three elements, in fact, are just about the right amount of time to move forward into Station 3.

Medium Platform w/Extension	KL-1003482-002		Stn:	2
Station 2: Tighten Frame X-Member		Line: B17	Mins/Stn:	2.332
	Element Description			Mins.
4	Assemble Frame Cross-Member to Frame w/(16) Screws			1.011
6	Tighten (16) Cross-Member Screws w/Power Tool			0.521
7	Torque (16) Cross-Member Screws and Mark			0.589
8	Assemble Valve Mounting Plate to Frame w/(4) Screws - w/Power Tool			0..466
~~9~~	~~Torque (4) Mounting Plate Screws and Mark~~			~~0.329~~
~~10~~	~~Mount Cylinder Valve to Mtg Plate w/(3) Screws~~			~~0.401~~
~~11~~	~~Torque (2) Cylinder Valve Screws and Mark~~			~~0.189~~
12	Advance Unit to Station 3	Fig 3-5-2		0.211

The result of moves into and out of Station 2 is: 2.240 mins + 1.011 - (.329+.401+.189) = 2.332 mins.

With the additions of Elements 9, 10, and 11, Station 3 time becomes 3.053, and it becomes the new bottleneck. However, Elements 16 and 17 can be easily performed in Station 4, and are thus moved.

Medium Platform w/Extension	KL-1003482-002		Stn:	3
Station 3: Hydraulic Tubes		Line: B17	Mins/Stn:	2.140
Element Description				Mins.
9	Torque (4) Mounting Plate Screws and Mark			0.329
10	Mount Cylinder Valve to Mtg Plate w/(3) Screws			0.401
11	Torque (2) Cylinder Valve Screws and Mark			0.189
13	Loose Assemble (2) Hydr Tube Clamps to Frame R/S Wall			0.363
14	Position (2) Hydr Tubes into R/S Wall Clamps			0.281
15	Align (2) Tubes and tighten (2) Clamps w/Power Tool			0.366
~~16~~	~~Asbl Supply Hose from Valve (Port A) to Upper Hydr Tube (Aft End) and Tig~~			~~0.457~~
~~17~~	~~Asbl Return Hose from Valve (Port B) to Lower Hydr Tube (Aft End) and Tig~~			~~0.457~~
18	Advance Unit to Station 4 Fig 3-5-3			0.211

The result of moves into and out of Station 3 is: 2.135 mins + (.329+.401+.189) - (.457+.457) = 2.140 mins.

And finally, moving Elements 16 and 17 makes Station 4 the new bottleneck at 3.058 minutes.

Medium Platform w/Extension	KL-1003482-002		Stn:	4
Station 4: Final Assy		Line: B17	Mins/Stn:	3.058
Element Description				Mins.
16	Asbl Supply Hose from Valve (Port A) to Upper Hydr Tube (Aft End) and Tig			0.457
17	Asbl Return Hose from Valve (Port B) to Lower Hydr Tube (Aft End) and Tig			0.457
19	Assemble R/S Extension Support to top of Frame w/(2) Screws			0.378
20	Assemble L/S Extension Support to top of Frame w/(2) Screws			0.378
21	Torque (4) Extension Support Screws and Mark			0.519
22	Torque (2) Hydr Hose Connectors (Both Ends) and Mark			0.389
23	Mark Sub-Assembly Sequence Number to Frame			0.178
24	Move Completed Sub-Assembly to Main Line Queue and Return Fig 3-5-4			0.302

The leveling process will sometimes require (or allow) fewer iterations than our simple example here. More likely, it will require more. It is largely a matter of how many work stations are on the line and what limitations do or do not exist. The leveling process will refine the balances of station times as much as is possible—*without altering the linear sequence.*

This, I believe, is important, because the process, as defined in the original sequence of events, was developed and determined to be the most efficient method of assembling the product. The leveling process will, in all likelihood, not get you to the final balance. But it will get you closer. Completing the second step in the balancing process brings us to the end game—actually solving the puzzle and producing the final and most efficient *balance* of work.

Looking at the graph, it would appear that all we have accomplished is to move a large bottleneck from the beginning to the end of the line. But there is more benefit here than it might seem. There is now flexibility in moving elements, which was not previously available. With Step Two completed, we now have a new base from which to begin to create the final balance. The results of the leveling exercise—and the starting point for Step Three are shown in Fig. 3-6, below:

Operation Balance Summary - Step 2				
Medium Platform w/Extension				
Station(s)	Mins/ Stn	+/- Avg Mins	% of Avg	Mins - Hi Stn
1-Load Frame	2.136	-.281	-11.6	.92
2-Tighten Frame	2.332	-.085	-3.5	.73
3-Hydr Tubes	2.140	-.277	-11.4	.92
4-Final Assy	3.058	.642	26.5	.00
Total Mins (TWC):	9.666	**Hi Stn**		
No of Stations:	4	**3.06**		
Avg. Mins:	**2.417**			
Takt Time =	2.700			
Avg. +/- Takt:	-.284			

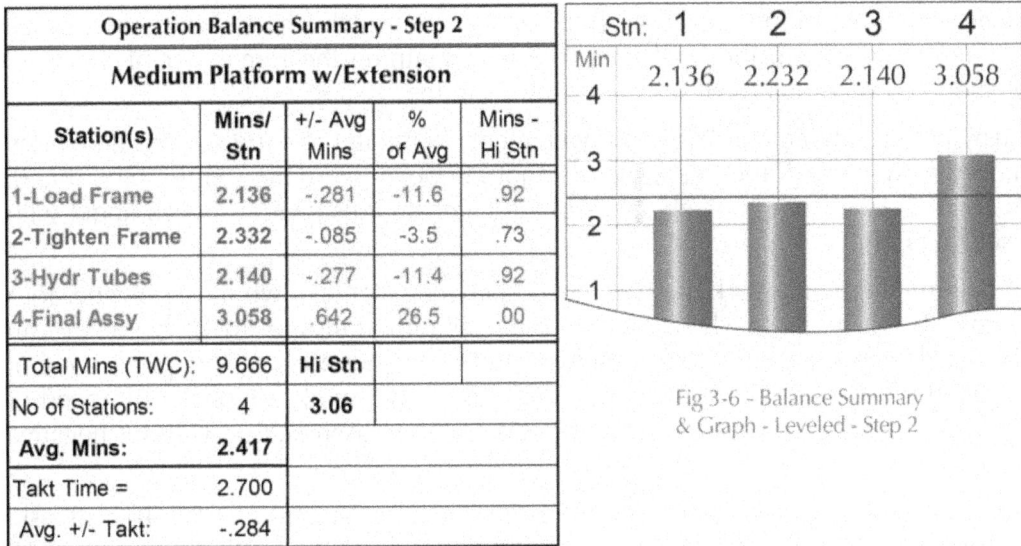

Stn:	1	2	3	4
	2.136	2.232	2.140	3.058

Fig 3-6 – Balance Summary & Graph - Leveled - Step 2

Before moving on to the final balance exercise—for the sake of clarity—I believe that it is a good idea to re-number the work station elements. In our example, we have done so.

Step Three: The Final Balance—Solving the Puzzle

A cautionary note at this point. Now that we are starting to move elements around, we will be revising the original sequence. In doing so, it is possible to disrupt or to reduce the inherent efficiency of the original process. This does not necessarily need to be so, but care should be taken to avoid or minimize such disruption.

A quick review of the Step Two balance data shows that the total assigned time in Station 2 is now within the +/- 5% limit. So, unless it proves impossible to achieve a successful balance among the remaining work stations, we will consider Station 2 to now be complete, as it is.

The next thing the data and the graph tell us is that Station 4 is now the bottleneck, and so our efforts will begin there.

It was earlier noted that most of what was accomplished in Step Two was to merely move the bottleneck from Station 1 to Station 4. Actually, this result is significantly more important than it might at first appear.

In Step One, establishing the work content of each station causes the initial stations to contain assigned times close to, or often slightly above average minutes. A reason for this is that, on many lines, the process tends to be "front-loaded." The early elements usually include the major structural components, with longer elemental times. This can make it difficult to establish the station break within the average minute boundary.

Stations closer to the line's finish tend to contain elements with lower elemental times, such as covers, trim pieces, plates, and decals. These generally smaller elemental times allow for station breaks to be established closer to average minutes. In addition, the final line station, containing the remainder of the work elements, is very often well under average minutes.

Many of the "fundamental" assembly elements found in the early stations cannot be moved forward or, if they can, they cannot be moved very far. On the other hand, many of the "finishing up" elements in the latter stations can be moved about with some freedom.

In determining what work may be moved between stations, we must consider four factors. The first, obviously, is time. But just as important are the other three. Can the selected work elements be removed from the sequence at this point without negatively impacting the remaining work? Also, what work stations are in need of time? And finally, can this work be placed to the chosen station without negative effect?

So, to begin Step Three, we look first to the bottleneck—Station 4—and ask, "Approximately how much time must be removed from the bottleneck, what work represents that time, and where could it go?".

Medium Platform w/Extension	KL-1003482-002		Stn:	4
Station 4: Extension Mounts		Line: B17	Mins/Stn:	2.302
Element Description				Mins.
17	Asbl Supply Hose from Valve (Port A) to Upper Hydr Tube (Aft End) and Tighten			0.457
18	Asbl Return Hose from Valve (Port B) to Lower Hydr Tube (Aft End) and Tighten			0.457
19	Assemble R/S Extension Support to top of Frame w/(2) Screws			0.378
20	Assemble L/S Extension Support to top of Frame w/(2) Screws			0.378
21	Torque (4) Extension Support Screws and Mark			0.519
22	Torque (2) Hydr Hose Connectors (Both Ends) and Mark			0.389
23	Mark Sub-Assembly Sequence Number to Frame			0.178
24	Move Completed Sub-Assembly to Main Line Queue and Return Fig 3-7-1			0.302

From a review of the work content and the sequence imperatives, it looks as if moving elements 19 and 20 (R/S and L/S extension supports) from Station 4 represents the right amount of time, and upon consideration is work that can be done anywhere after the initial loading of the frame to the line. Finally, moving this work into Station 1 will not interfere with any part of the process in Station 1 itself or as the unit moves forward.

The result of moves out of Station 4 is: 3.058 mins - (.378 + .378) = 2.302 mins.

Station 4's total time is now within the +/- 5% limit, so we will consider it to be complete.

The result of moves into Station 1 is: 2.136 mins - (.378 + .378) = 2.892 mins. This is better than Station 1's original time, but the addition of this work makes Station 1 again the bottleneck, so that is where we next turn our attention.

Once again we ask the question, "What can now be moved from Station 1 without negative consequence?".

We don't need much time, and the attachment of the nameplate can be done virtually anywhere. But where to move it to? We have undertaken not to alter Station 2 unless absolutely necessary, and Station 4 is, at least for the moment, done. So let's consider the effect of moving it to Station 3.

Medium Platform w/Extension KL-1003482-002		Stn:	1
Station 1: Mount Frame to Line	**Line: B17**	**Mins/Stn:**	**2.892**
Element Description			Mins.
1	Load Frame from Queue to Line Work Station 1 w/Hoist		1.321
~~2~~	~~Attach Nameplate to Frame w/(4) Pop Rivits~~		~~0.381~~
3	Attach Logo Plate to Frame w/(2) Pop Rivits		0.223
19	Assemble R/S Extension Support to top of Frame w/(2) Screws		0.378
20	Assemble L/S Extension Support to top of Frame w/(2) Screws		0.378
4	Advance Unit to Station 2	Fig 3-7-2	0.211

The result of previous moves into Station 1 is: 2.126 mins + (.378 + .378) = 2.892 mins.

As had been determined, moving the attachment of the nameplate to the frame is acceptable, both in time and work sequence. The result of moving the nameplate out of Station 1 is: 2.892 mins - .381 = 2.511 mins. This means that Station 1 is now within the +/- 5% limit.

Medium Platform w/Extension		KL-1003482-002		Stn:	3
Station 3: Hydraulic Tubes			Line: B17	Mins/Stn:	2.521
Element Description					Mins.
10	Torque (4) Mounting Plate Screws and Mark				0.329
2	Attach Nameplate to Frame w/(4) Pop Rivits				0.381
11	Mount Cylinder Valve to Mtg Plate w/(3) Screws				0.401
12	Torque (2) Cylinder Valve Screws and Mark				0.189
13	Loose Assemble (2) Hydr Tube Clamps to Frame R/S Wall				0.363
14	Position (2) Hydr Tubes into R/S Wall Clamps				0.281
15	Align (2) Tubes and tighten (2) Clamps w/Power Tool				0.366
16	Advance Unit to Station 4			Fig 3-7-3	0.211

The result of moving the nameplate into Station 3 is: 2.140 mins + .381 = 2.521 mins. This brings Station 3 into the limit—and we are done!

The final results of Steps 1, 2, and finally 3 are shown in the data and graph below.

Operation Balance Summary				
Medium Platform w/Extension				
Station(s)	Mins/ Stn	+/- Avg Mins	% of Avg	Mins - Hi Stn
1-Load Frame	2.511	.095	3.9	.01
2-Tighten Frame	2.332	-.085	-3.5	.19
3-Hydr Tubes	2.521	.105	4.3	.00
4- Final Assy	2.302	-.115	-4.7	.22
Total Mins (TWC):	9.666	Hi Stn		
No of Stations:	4	2.521		
Avg. Mins:	2.417			
Takt Time =	2.700			
Avg. +/- Takt:	-.284			

Stn:	1	2	3	4
Min	2.511	2.332	2.521	2.302

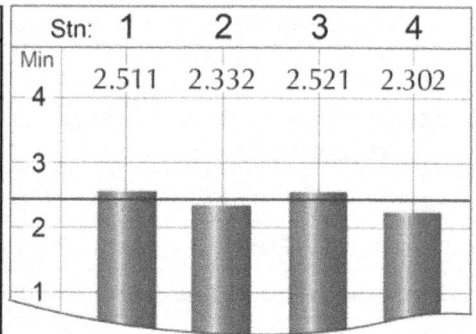

Fig 3-8 - Balance Summary
& Graph - Final Balance - Step 3

Final Thoughts

The foregoing example of the three-step process of assembly line balancing is admittedly a simple one, but I believe that it embodies a demonstration of principles and methodology that are applicable to any line, of any level of complexity.

Steps One and Two are straightforward and somewhat mechanical exercises, which set the stage for the final step, namely the final balance solution, which requires the creative application of "what if?" and the literal give-and-take that solves the puzzle.

Creating the final balance can be as simple as the example above, or it may be a difficult and grueling process—as good puzzles often are. However, with preparation, as outlined in Parts One and Two, and a thorough understanding of the subject process that is wrought by this preparation, I have complete faith that the solution is always in there somewhere, just waiting to be revealed.

5. Exploiting the Balance

Introduction

A balance—the written documentation provided by the sequence of events—is now organized into a multi-station, synchronous, linear process. A process capable, when implemented and properly managed, of achieving the desired production goal is, to say the least, quite a good thing for an assembly organization to have. The balance therefore, in and of itself, is a valuable tool. But this collection of manufacturing process information, in its present form, has the potential to be much more.

In addition to being a balance, the documentation offers a simple instruction, spelling out precisely where and how required work is (or at least should be) performed and, importantly, how long it should take. This is vital information. The balance not only defines the work sequence and method but is also the basis of the work standard. The standard in turn is a key factor in determining material supply, completion, and shipping schedules, and, of course, labor cost.

Appending Manufacturing Information

I stated earlier that the completed, balanced sequence of work elements, organized over a series of specific locations, can become the repository for all or any part of the manufacturing information associated with building the product, organized in the sequence in which the product is assembled.

Additional information supplemental to the building of that product may, via the elemental task list in the balance, be appended to and associated discretely with each work station or, perhaps more importantly, to individual tasks within each work station. And if—and when—the sequence is re-organized (a revised balance), all attached data is automatically re-organized as well.

Typically, the first of this supplemental information is materials, i.e., the component parts of the assembly, which must be delivered to precise locations and at specific times. Attached material data can provide "where used" parts lists; extremely valuable in the management of materials. "Where used" lists may contain part numbers, quantities, and delivery locations, in fact, any bit of information desired regarding the assembly's component parts and where they are consumed.

Similarly, tools lists, again organized and documented by work station or task, allow tooling or equipment management to know precisely what is needed and where.

Next on the list of desirable additional information are "work instructions," variously known as operational method sheets (OMS's), operational instruction sheets (OIS's), or in fact anything the local management might choose to call them —Including the often-used term "standard work," though, in the strictest sense, standard work is something a bit different. However, as long as everyone in a given organization knows what the term means, any term is good enough.

Regardless of what they're called, work instructions, written or graphic (or ideally both), are a valuable addition to the shop floor environment. Experienced team members usually don't need them on a daily basis, but having detailed assembly instructions, written in plain, easily, and quickly understandable form, are a handy reference and are extremely helpful in training new associates.

"Grouping Elements"

While helpful in balancing, the concept of the smallest transferable element is inconvenient when using the completed balanced sequence of events as instruction, or for helping to create a manageable and coherent set of graphic instructions. Now that elemental assignments are fixed, individual work elements may be combined or "grouped" into larger, complete tasks.

For example, in Part One we discussed the assembly of hydraulic tubes and clamps to the side wall of a unit. Tightening and torqueing the clamps were listed as discrete assembly steps, allowing the possibility of performing some or all of that work at a later station.

However, once it has been determined that the complete task—assembly, tightening fasteners, and torqueing—are to be done in one work station, the sequence of events may be revised, and times combined, to list this work as a single element.

"Assemble, Clamp, and Tighten (2) Hydr Tubes to Left Side Wall—Torque and Mark".

Take another example of element grouping. A sequence of events lists the connections of 10 wires to a terminal block. Each wire connection represents a discrete element of work, each with a time of .087 minutes. Any one, or any combination, of these 10 wires may potentially be connected in any of several work stations (a perfect example of the "balancers," which were discussed in the previous section).

These 10 wires, and a sum of 1.87 mins, appear in the sequence of events and are assigned as follows to Station 4:

Route and Connect RED Wire (23) to Terminal Block-1 (Terminal 1A) .187
Route and Connect BLACK Wire (46) to Terminal Block-1 (Terminal 3A) .187
Route and Connect BLUE Wire (18) to Terminal Block-1 (Terminal 5A) .187
Route and Connect YELLOW Wire (32) to Terminal Block-1 (Terminal 1B) .187
Route and Connect PURPLE Wire (38) to Terminal Block-1 (Terminal 2B) .187
Route and Connect TAN Wire (44) to Terminal Block-1 (Terminal 8A) .187
Route and Connect WHITE Wire (27) to Terminal Block-1 (Terminal 6B) .187
Route and Connect GREY Wire (23) to Terminal Block-1 (Terminal 7B) .187
Route and Connect ORANGE Wire (31) to Terminal Block-1 (Terminal 8B) .187
Route and Connect GREEN Wire (44) to Terminal Block-1 (Terminal GND) .187

As a result of the balance, 1.22 minutes were removed from Station 4 and distributed to the next three work stations. Instead of 10 individual line items, the sequence now includes the following elements within the various work stations to which the work has been reassigned:

Station 4: *Route and Connect (4) Wires to Terminal Block-1*   *.748*
  RED (23 to Terminal 1A
  BLACK to (46) to Terminal 3A
  BLUE (18 to Terminal 1A
  YELLOW (32 to Terminal 1A

Station 5: *Route and Connect (4) Wires to Terminal Block-1*   *.374*
  PURPLE Wire (38) to Terminal 2B
  TAN Wire (44) to Terminal 8A

Station 6: *Route and Connect (2) Wires to Terminal Block-1*   *.561*
  WHITE to (27) to Terminal 6B
  GREY Wire (23) to Terminal 7B
  ORANGE Wire (31) to Terminal 8B

Station 7: *Route and Connect GREEN Wire (44) to Terminal GND*   *.187*
  GREY Wire (23) to Terminal 7B

In this hypothetical example of fine-tuning the process, documentation has been accomplished by moving six of the "smallest transferable elements" to different work stations, and, once their final location has been determined, the elemental list has been simplified by combining or "grouping" the elements into single line items.

As to graphic instructions, 10 individual instructions would be obviously cumbersome and impractical. However, a single instruction at each work station showing which of the 10 wires are connected at that location is clear and concise.

Author's note: Grouping elements is a powerful tool, but I would strongly advise maintaining a copy of the original balanced sequence of events, retaining the ability to "ungroup" these elements if and when a re-balance is required.

Afterword

This book began as an idea for a simple magazine article or perhaps a pamphlet, offering the fundamentals of assembly line balance, as well as my approach and methods regarding the balance process, which have permitted me some success over the years.

It soon became obvious, however, that there was more to the story. A lot more. Having read this far, you've certainly heard me express repeatedly, when it comes to most IE tasks, my belief in the paramountcy of understanding the basic sequence of any given process. Part One of this book deals with this fundamental issue.

Simply put, the heart of the balancing process itself is the movement of bits of time. This leads to Part Two, which concerns itself not so much with the mechanics of work measurement, but with the engineer's approach to the task of doing work measurement. This relates to the human interaction between the industrial engineer and the skilled, intelligent shop-floor associates who often really don't want you to be there, doing what you are doing. It also relates to my belief that, if you *are* going to be out there, doing work measurement, it must be done fairly.

And finally the payoff, Part Three: the information and the calculations required to set up the puzzle, and a discussion of the methodologies by which we find the solution.

I long ago came to the realization that my ways, however successful, are not the *only* ways. What I do and how I do it are an amalgam of what I have learned from a number of sources, including some pretty good mentors, some formal training, and a few things I dreamed up on my own. Added to this of course is the passage of time, during which I mostly tried to pay attention.

So, I offer this book as one of perhaps many sources which you may find helpful. May your sequences be complete, your times accurate, and your lines well-balanced.

Tom Shropshire